PSYCHOLOGY
AS SCIENCE
AND ART

PSYCHOLOGY AS SCIENCE AND ART

JAMES DEESE
The Johns Hopkins University

Under the General Editorship of
Jerome Kagan, Harvard University

HARCOURT BRACE JOVANOVICH, INC.
New York   Chicago   San Francisco   Atlanta

ISBN: 0-15-572967-5

Library of Congress Catalog Card Number: 79-188793

Printed in the United States of America

PREFACE

Another book about how psychology is truly scientific? Not quite. Some psychological knowledge *is* scientific—it comes from general principles that in turn are based on reliable experience. Some psychological knowledge, however, comes from uncodified, intuitive experience, and that part is art. In all science there is more art than the layman or the casual student would be led to expect from accounts of the philosophy of science, and psychology is no exception. Furthermore, a great portion of human knowledge is in the form of myth, and again knowledge about psychology is no exception. So, this book is about how psychology is both a science and an art and how psychological knowledge is a mixture of science and myth. It doesn't take the position that this mixture is necessarily good or bad, only that we should recognize it as such if we are going to understand modern psychology and its uses.

The reader need not know very much about psychology to understand this book. Occasional references to ideas and facts that may be puzzling should not prevent the student from following the important arguments. (He may want to make use of a comprehensive introductory textbook in psychology to become better acquainted with unfamiliar concepts.) The chapters may be read separately and independently. Thus, the student who simply wants an overview of contemporary psychology can read only the last chapter. The first three chapters deal with the scientific method in psychology in greatest detail and should be of primary interest to those concerned with this subject.

This book is not meant to be learned or memorized. It may have to be studied, for it presents ideas that are subtle and complicated. But it should be studied as an essay, not as a textbook. The facts that it contains are only incidental to the issues it raises, for this is a book meant to be discussed, argued, and perhaps dis-

v

agreed with. No final answers or easily summarized principles are provided. There is a point of view about philosophy of science and some probing of the soft spots in modern psychology based on this point of view. The major purpose of this probing is to give the student an understanding of the difficulties of obtaining psychological knowledge, respect for the knowledge we do have, and, perhaps, some motivation to look for better ways of acquiring this kind of knowledge.

For their helpful responses to various portions of the manuscript I would like to thank Jerome Kagan, Harvard University; Edward Murray, University of Miami; and Richard L. Solomon, University of Pennsylvania.

JAMES DEESE

CONTENTS

1
PSYCHOLOGY AS SCIENCE

Psychology is in a state of crisis. That crisis has revealed itself ominously in the growing distrust in the scientific method generally and in the experimental method in particular. This distrust is to be found among all kinds of people concerned with psychological problems, from students to practitioners and investigators. Although most textbooks in psychology continue to present the traditional views about psychology as a science, almost no one, not even those who write those books, entirely believes them anymore. The traditional views are seen, at best, only as half-truths. The result is a widespread feeling of futility among students of psychology and even among some professional psychologists. Some people find enough things wrong with the current state of psychology to say that we should abandon the whole scientific enterprise in psychology and frankly admit that it must be compounded of myth and fantasy. Such counsel is wrong, for a number of reasons, but equally wrong is the hope that if we proclaim outmoded slogans loud and long enough they might be believed. We might be better advised to see where the scientific method in psychology leads and how it is, often in practice, supplemented by art and skill.

Most psychologists take it as an article of faith that psychology is a science. A determined but small minority insists that it is not, and this minority most often pledges its loyalty to something called humanism. The term "humanism" like the term "science" is easily misused. Among humanistic psychologists it seems to mean that psychological knowledge, some of which comes from intuition and

1

reflection rather than science, should be applied with particular ethical aims and moral values in mind. Humanism in psychology has come to be a kind of rallying point for an antiscientific attitude. The growing dispute between the scientific majority and the humanistic minority in psychology is alarming, and it should lead us to reconsider the nature of psychology as a science. Psychology both as science and as art depends on the assumption of certain ethical values, and these values can be compatible with humanistic values. In order to see that scientific psychology is as much committed to values as humanistic psychology, however, it is necessary to adopt a new attitude toward the philosophy of science and psychology's relation to it. One of the purposes of this book is to offer a new attitude.

The philosophy of science

Science, in its simplest and most fundamental sense, means knowledge. Any particular science is simply a department of systematized knowledge. Given that definition, there should be little doubt that much of contemporary psychology is respectably scientific. But science has come in the twentieth century to be more than just a synonym for reliable human knowledge. It has come to mean knowledge of a particular sort obtained in particular ways. This specialized interpretation of the word "science" is exemplified by the enormous success of the physical sciences. Science has almost come to mean, in its most restricted sense, physics and chemistry, together with those methods, chiefly mathematical and experimental, that establish the generalities on which the familiar, though mysterious, miracles of twentieth-century technology are based.

In the past quarter of a century, biology has moved to full membership in the inner circle of scientific reputability. The reason for this development is not that the biological knowledge of the present is essentially more reliable than that of twenty-five years ago. It is simply that modern biology has become more like physics and chemistry. This development in biology has resulted from a genuine step forward in human knowledge. It has meant that we have a much better understanding of the physical basis of life. But this development has produced a neglect of certain aspects of biology that from a standpoint of human values and knowledge are important. For example, ecology, which is concerned with the place of life in the natural scheme of things, is an aspect of biological science that is nonphysical in its methods and basic conceptions. Ecology does not rely on physical theory so much as it does on statistics and the theory of systems. Until the recent concern with the quality of the environment arose, ecology was a neglected aspect of biology.

For many years, a large and active group of psychologists worked hard to make psychology over in the image of physics. Their effort took several forms. In its best and most fruitful form, it took the role of experimental explorations on the borderline between psychology and physiology (and ultimately in the physics of organisms). These efforts worked in the interests of the unity of sciences. They were aimed at the development of comprehensive knowledge and an understanding of the relation of the mind to its physical substrate. This enterprise was and is one of the richest and most valuable in the whole spectrum of the psychological sciences.

Less valuable has been the blind transfer of the conceptual apparatus of the physical sciences to psychology as a whole. This wholesale transfer is evident in innumerable ways—in certain kinds of psychological theories (which are usually stated in analytic mathematical form), in reliance on statistical inference, in the preeminence of the notion of experiment, and in the common use of terms like "independent and dependent variable" to describe the form of scientific exploration in psychology. Of course the commitment goes deeper than these superficial characteristics. A very significant portion of those psychologists who are leaders in scientific research follow, in some instances almost blindly, a theory of scientific method that represents a philosophic formalization of the methods of late nineteenth- and early twentieth-century physics. Many of these psychologists believe that the development of the main outlines of scientific method stopped in the second quarter of the twentieth century.

The early years of the twentieth century saw the most brilliant development of the philosophy of science. Two ideas that developed during this period had an especially important effect on psychology. These were *logical positivism* and *operationalism*. Logical positivism is the view that science is a coherent series of statements and arguments concerned only with empirical knowledge, that which is obtained by observation. It is logical because it attempts to be coherent and free from internal contradiction. It is positivistic in that it rejects any metaphysical explanation. Operationalism is similar, but it is more concerned with the immediate matter of making scientific observations and limiting scientific statements to what can be said about observable events. Both logical positivism and operationalism were largely negative in their intent. They were meant to discourage scientists from embarking on scientifically useless enterprises. They were important ideas, but they have outlived much of their usefulness in psychology. In no small measure, the persistence of the point of view associated with these positions is responsible for today's crisis, for the sense of futility and panic that now assails some psychologists. The climate of opinion created by these ideas has become inhibiting to scientific progress in several aspects of psychology. It has produced a shibboleth to which the student must subscribe in order to join in the scientific psychological enterprise. An increasing number of students simply refuse to do so; many have become interested in something else—for example, the view that psychology is not and cannot be a science. The result of this reaction has been to inject into contemporary psychology a certain measure of anti-intellectualism and antirationalism, and this reaction is something that is disturbing to those of us who teach psychology.

Nearly everyone agrees that science is concerned with the search for verifiable truth or for reliable knowledge. It is more difficult, however, to characterize truth and knowledge as the scientist views them. The main tradition of positivism in the philosophy of science rejects any metaphysical notion of truth or knowledge. Instead, the criteria of truth or knowledge center on issues of consistency and empirical verifiability. Introductory accounts of the philosophy of science in psychology textbooks often characterize science as a kind of game. Games must have some consistency or they cannot be played. But games differ in the extent to which they may be explained and their outcomes predicted. Some games are entirely abstract. Chess is such a game. Some other games, such as football, are not abstract. In chess all possible games, in theory, can be stated beforehand, but they cannot be in football; the football game *must* be played if one is to know the outcome. Chess is totally consistent; football is not. Hence referees are not necessary in chess. If science can be characterized as a game, it is somewhere in between, although it is closer to football than to chess. There is no mechanical way to play the game of science, for science isn't completely formal—it has some unpredictable aspects. As in all games, however, there are rules, and these rules are necessary if the game is to be played in such a way as to make sense.

The scientific method

Rules serve to keep games free of internal contradictions. The rules in chess, for example, serve to define possible moves. The various moves can be characterized in a kind of algebraic notation for which the chessmen on a checkerboard are an unnecessary manifestation. In one view of the philosophy of science, empirical information (information obtained by direct observation) serves a function similar to that of the chessmen: scientific observations are simply concrete ways of realizing the possible results that stem from the application of an internally consistent set of rules. This view of science as verging on the abstract is not a popular one among practicing scientists, but it is common among philosophers of science and certain theorists in psychology. However, since science, unlike chess, is not a completely predictable game, there will be outcomes in science that are unexpected. The rules of science are not sufficient to tell us what all the possible outcomes of scientific investigation will be. That is why there is discovery in science.

The classical account of the scientific method specifies three steps: (1) the formation of hypotheses, (2) the empirical testing of the hypotheses, and (3) the acceptance or rejection of the hypotheses. A scientific investigation is supposed to begin with a collection of hypothetical statements, at least some of which can be tested by experiment or observation. The purpose of experimentation, then, is to see whether or not those hypotheses are true in some particular cases. In short, experimenting provides an empirical test for some of the hypotheses. If the results of the tests are positive, the hypothetical propositions are said to be more plausible. This leap from data to verification, supposedly the direct outcome of results in the laboratory, is a rather vague step as specified by psychologists. That psychologists slide over it rather quickly, however, should not blind us to the fact that it is a profound issue in the philosophy of science for it is the heart of *induction*, the production of specific facts to prove a general statement. Induction—as philosophers from David Hume (an eighteenth-century Scottish philosopher) to the present have noted—has a very strange status in any purely rational enterprise. To some philosophers induction does not seem to have any thoroughly rational basis. Therefore, because science is said to be rational and logical, induction remains a kind of whale among fishes in the philosophy of science. But no matter what their views are on the philosophy of science, all scientists accept on faith the proposition that knowledge may be increased through induction. The need to generalize from particular facts to universal laws is the sole reason why science is not purely rational. Induction distinguishes science from mathematics.

The theory of the scientific method to be found in most introductory textbooks in psychology states that the first step in a scientific investigation is to find some good hypotheses. This often calls on the rules of logic, because propositions embodying the hypotheses must be stated and their implications derived in logical form if science is to be truly rigorous. The oldest and best-known applications of logic are in traditional fields of mathematics. Mathematics in the service of scientific hypotheses is one of the great glories of the physical sciences. Some psychologists have envied the ability of physicists to use mathematics in deriving testable hypotheses and have sought to use the same methods in the formation of psychological hypotheses. As a result, some psychological theories are almost indistinguishable in form from physical theories. The arguments are stated as definitions and postulates that lead, through mathematical argument, to theorems. Some of the theorems turn out to be testable. Testable theorems are propositions that can be paralleled by events observed in the laboratory or in nature. This makes possible the second stage in the traditional account of scientific investigation. If the theoretical argument is stated in classical mathematical form, the empirical tests of the hypothesis must be similarly stated. Thus, quantification, scales of measurement, and number have generally become important if not absolutely central to certain branches of empirical psychology.

Associated with this pressure toward quantification is a way of conceiving psychological experimentation or observation that also comes from elementary mathematics. Those who have studied any psychology at all will be familiar with the characterization of psychological observations as "variables." Those variables that are said to be under the control of the person performing experiments are *independent variables,* and those variables that change in reaction to the independent variables are the *dependent variables.* In much psychological theory of the past generation, dependent variables have been identified with various responses of organisms, while the independent variables have been identified with the stimuli that impinge upon those organisms. This kind of analysis is particularly compatible with psychology's *stimulus-response theory.* There is an important relation between the traditional account of the scientific method in psychology and stimulus-response theory, which will be examined in due course.

The final stage in the traditional account of scientific investigation is the acceptance or rejection of the relevant hypotheses. Hypotheses can be confirmed or disconfirmed, depending on how closely they accord with the observed measurements. Statistical analysis helps determine whether or not the results are reliable and hence whether or not it is possible to confirm or disconfirm from the empirical results. There is a great deal of confusion attending the problem of precisely when an exact formulation of an hypothesis is confirmed or disconfirmed. Once accomplished, however, the confirmation of a number of hypotheses is supposed to make the theory from which the hypotheses are derived acceptable. In the traditional view, a good scientific theory is one that generates many testable hypotheses. The traditional point of view also has it that if enough hypotheses are correct, the theory should be accepted. Thus, the theory acquires truth by a kind of vote, a vote not obtained by public opinion but by how many hypothetical outcomes are in accord with actual observations. The fact that in the history of science no scientific theory has been accepted or rejected for a considerable period of time on this basis does not disturb those who argue for this point of view.

Operationalism: the scientific method in psychology in practice

Buried in the traditional account of the application of scientific method to psychology are several problems. One is the identification of measurable psychological variables with the abstract mathematical notation that arises from a theory. Quantitative theory may be stated in ordinary algebraic equations or in differential form, and even theory that is not by tradition quantitative may be stated in a mathematical way. In the most advanced scientific theories, the form of the argument is abstract and developed in some logical or mathematical notation. In order to apply the theory to the real world, it is necessary to identify elements of the abstract notation with the observation of particular events in the natural world. The easy way to accomplish this is through the hocus-pocus of *operationalism*.

Operationalism is the traditional formula by which the abstractions of theory are transmuted into something that has psychological significance and in turn by which the psychologically significant thing is transmuted into something observable. For example, an abstract relation might be stated as:

$$A = I \times M$$

This statement has no psychological significance, although by invoking the rules of algebra, it can be made to generate certain other abstract statements, such as:

$$I = \frac{A}{M}$$

Psychological significance can be granted by making A equal to achievement, I to intelligence, and M to motivation. Achievement is the "dependent variable" and intelligence and motivation the "independent variables." The problem is to specify achievement, intelligence, and motivation in a way that permits their evaluation or measurement. If that is done, it might be argued, we would have a theoretical hypothesis that could be investigated empirically and subjected to scientific test.

The statement implied by the equation says, among other things, that both intelligence and motivation are necessary for achievement. It has some common sense that lends it a certain a priori plausibility (a condition that is more important to empirical psychologists than many of them would like to admit). A problem arises, however, when we try to "measure" intelligence and motivation. One solution—all too easy—is to identify each of the terms with something already measured. We have intelligence tests; therefore, intelligence tests measure intelligence. No matter that we don't know exactly how or why they measure intelligence; it is sufficient to know there are things called intelligence tests. Motivation is a little more difficult, but it does not present insuperable difficulties. Psychologists measure a certain kind of motivation through something they call *n*-achievement, which is determined by means of a test consisting of stories people tell in response to certain pictures (the Thematic Apperception Test). How do we measure achievement? The operational interpretation of the formula tells us that we multiply intelligence scores by *n*-achievement scores to get an achievement measure. In the interests of tidiness, we shall have to find the appropriate "scale factors" or constants by which to reduce the test scores to sets of convenient measures.

We have, by fiat, measured achievement. We still do not know, however, whether our measurement is useful. So we may try to "validate" the measure. The validation is achieved by yet another resort to operational magic. We say achievement is evidenced by college grades. So we then *correlate* our measure, based on the product of intelligence test scores and *n*-achievement scores with college grades, and lo and behold, in a sample of 257 individuals we achieve a correlation "significant at the .05 level." [1] No matter

---

[1] Empirical results in psychology, as in all sciences, are supposed to be reliable. Statistical tests have been invented for the purpose of determining

that nearly every psychological measurement that one can think of may be correlated with every other measure. No matter the severe restrictions on inferences that are drawn from correlations. What we may think we have accomplished is to verify a theoretical proposition. At best what our example may have accomplished is a low grade of psychometric engineering and at worst a systematic fraud. Any one of an incredibly large range of hypotheses could be "verified" by the same procedure. Such magic and illusion are all too common in psychology. In fact, one finds that such thinking so permeates psychological theory that it is difficult to write a coherent account of almost any area in psychology without resorting to such a procedure in the name of psychological theory and hypothesis testing.

This procedure substitutes the appearance of rigor for explicit theoretical derivation. The exhibition of a correlation between intelligence test scores, *n*-achievement scores, and college grades is a contribution, however modest, to knowledge. But masquerading, under the guise of operationalism, as the examination of a theory about how ability and achievement work, it can only be regarded as a delusion. The delusion is puffed up to grand proportions by borrowing the meaning of the concepts of intelligence and motivation as they occur in everyday usage. There is no theory, in the sense of an explicit and non-self-contradictory system, but only the appearance of one. Or, if it is a theory, it is one that, for all its elaborate framework, supports only a small structure of facts.

The apparatus of quantification has been put in the service of disguising poorly realized conceptions, such as the one (implicit in the above discussion) that motivation is something that varies only in amount. If we stop and think about the implications of "amount" of motivation or of achievement, the potential absurdity of the notion becomes apparent. It implies that the Peace Corps volunteer's motivation and the champion tennis player's are made in the same way, differing, if at all, only in amount. This may be, but the implications are far more general than any single empirical test of such a "theory" could verify. Applying the results of one

how much reliance can be placed on a particular outcome. The meaning of "significant at the .05 level" is subtle, but, in very loose terms, it tells us that some particular result is—in the most general case—reliable in some agreed upon minimal sense.

test to a whole range of interests and activities is so familiar to psychologists that they no longer regard it as absurd but as the very substance of psychological theory. To the person who is grounded in the explicit theorizing of the physical and mathematical sciences, it is usually surprising that the psychologist regards, for instance, a wish to do well in school to be equivalent in motivation to the desire to sell a million dollars worth of life insurance a year. They are both examples of motivation, perhaps, but the psychologist's confusion of them baffles the person used to genuine logical rigor.

Measurement and the mathematical and logical apparatus associated with it are of central importance in psychological theory. But these have suffered so from the too easy use of operationalism in much of psychological observation that they have lost their currency among some psychologists. Unfortunately, students, who often see through the sham of operationalism as practiced in much of modern psychology and advocated in all too many textbooks, sometimes condemn the whole apparatus of mathematics, genuine rigor, and appropriate quantification in psychology along with that which is obviously meretricious. One result has been that the revolt against the traditional doctrines of scientific method has been accompanied by a considerable measure of anti-intellectualism. The rational apparatus of science and the discovery of new knowledge have been mistakenly rejected because of their association with the *appearance* of the rational in psychological science.

Perhaps the most significant outcome of operationalism in psychology is the curious, but by now nearly universal, assumption that the subject matter of psychology is behavior. This assumption dates from before the formal introduction of operationalism. It stems from an insight made more than fifty years ago by the American psychologist John B. Watson. Watson developed a doctrine called *behaviorism*.[2] He argued that the psychologist, as a scientist, studied behavior, not the mind, or consciousness, which was supposed to be the traditional subject matter of psychology.

---

[2] The most influential book in the genesis of behaviorism was J. B. Watson, *Psychology from the Standpoint of a Behaviorist* (Philadelphia: Lippincott, 1919).

Psychologists studied behavior in order to predict and control it. Prediction and control were the pragmatic measures of success in psychological science. Watson thus swept aside difficult questions regarding the nature of knowledge, or epistemology, the curious status of direct observation, and the nature of experience. Watson's triumphant rebuilding of psychology along objective lines resulted in the spectacle of a whole generation of psychologists accepting the proposition that the subject matter of psychology is behavior.

It is now possible to see, however, that psychology is the science of behavior only in a trivial sense. It is so in the sense that physics is the science of meter reading and chemistry the science of observing changes in the color of paper. This identification of the subject matter of scientific investigation with what metering instruments and indicators detect is unique to what have come to be known as the behavioral sciences. In an attempt to escape the introspective subjectivity of pre-Watsonian experimental psychology, contemporary psychologists have embraced a new kind of subjectivism, confusing the notion of fact in the sense of knowledge with fact in the sense of a record of some observation. But from a standpoint of the ultimate subjectivity of knowledge, the way in which a needle swings on a psychogalvanometric apparatus is no less subjective than the peculiar nature of the sensation of the color green (the type of study favored by introspective pre-Watsonians). What is of ultimate significance is the fact for which the psychogalvanometric reaction stands. If it stands for no fact whatever, it has no more meaning than the most evanescent, private experience reported by the old-fashioned student of introspection.

The effort to stay the sterile subjectivism that was supposed to characterize prebehavioristic psychology, coupled with the acceptance of a philosophy of science appropriate to late nineteenth-century physics, has made some aspects of scientific psychology most unsatisfactory. It has produced a subject matter that is anti-theoretical, conservative, and intellectually unappealing—despite a commitment of most psychologists to scientific theory, to richness of fact, and to the development of new techniques.

The background
of modern psychology

In the Anglo-American academic tradition, psychology belongs to that branch of philosophy closest to ethics and theology. When, in the nineteenth century, those bold enough first announced themselves as psychological scientists at Oxford, Harvard, and Cambridge, they were in revolt against the quasi-theological position that psychology occupied in the traditional spectrum of learning in England, Scotland, and the United States. When early American psychologists attacked theologically based views of man, psychology, with some justification, became identified with the position of skepticism. The result is that by tradition psychologists feel it necessary to clear out of the house of the mind all the controversies that rage in the name of faith rather than in that of science and reason. Thus, psychologists have come to avoid questions of free will versus determinism, the nature of the soul, and the inextensibility of mind. They quite rightly regard these as questions for which the methods of science are no more powerful than the methods of rhetoric and disputation.

Psychologists have identified themselves with a different set of problems, those that arise from a scientific context. They concern the place of man's mind in nature, its relation to the animal mind and to the whole realm of natural being. In arguing that these questions were the subject matter of psychology, rather than those that occupied the moral philosophers and theologians, psychologists became propagandists. Those who wrote textbooks for the general audiences held that such propaganda was necessary. It has become almost universally accepted that one of the functions of instruction in psychology is to get the student to make a skeptical examination of outmoded beliefs. This enterprise was carried on in some textbooks to the point of reducing psychology to a mass of trivia. An earlier generation of scientific textbooks listed those preconceptions that students were supposed to have about ordinary things and said how these were wrong. Thus, students were told not only that disputes about free will versus determinism were in principle not answerable by empirical—that is, scientific—techniques, but that they must abandon beliefs that blondes are frivolous, that redheads are emotionally excitable, and that a person who can't look you in the eye can't be trusted. It was the function of at least one generation of psychology textbooks to disabuse students of the notion that geniuses are odder than people of average intelligence, that human behavior is instinctive, that people who learn slowly remember what they learn, and that the study of mathematics exercises the mind in such a way that a person who studies it can think more logically in other subjects. Some of these assertions are, of course, trivial and things about which students of an earlier generation, much less students of the contemporary sort, couldn't care less. Furthermore, in an eagerness to embrace objective method, psychologists were guilty of confusing their own beliefs with fact. Many of their "corrections" went beyond empirical fact, and still others were downright wrong.

This state of affairs was in considerable part the result of the central place occupied by experimental psychology in the scientific tradition of psychology. Experimental psychology was an invention of nineteenth-century Germany and in particular of Wilhelm Wundt. Nearly all the special scientific disciplines as we now know them arose in the academic environment of nineteenth-century Germany for the reason that the very notion of academic specialties developed in that environment. Experimental psychology's dual ancestry is German philosophy and physiology. The original purpose of experimental psychology was to study stimuli as they impinged on the mind. Nineteenth-century German experimental psychologists viewed their subject matter as the study of consciousness. They said they studied the content of the normal conscious mind. Contemporary experimental psychologists talk little about consciousness, but they talk a great deal about stimuli for reasons that lie in the nature of the experimental method itself. The experimental method, as it is applied in psychology, depends on the ability of the experimenter to control and change events independently of the human being who is the object of study. The early experimental psychologists produced stimuli and asked how their effects were reflected in the experience of their subjects. They studied, for example, the reactions of subjects to tones of different frequencies and to visual stimuli of different spectral compositions. Such stimuli are, for the most part, physically, or at least psychophysically, specifiable, and the achievement of producing and measuring them was one of the great accomplishments of early experimental psychology. Experimental psychology as the study of the reaction to stimuli (or, more properly, stimulus attributes) could rely on the high degree of precision that had been brought about by the nearly two hundred years of experimental physics following Newton.

Experimental psychology since the founding of the early laboratories in the last quarter of the nineteenth century has accumulated much information about how sense organs work and about how we experience our visual and auditory worlds. Some experiments in the study of associations and memory also came out of early laboratories, and these were occasionally interesting and provocative. With the extended development of information about sensory capacities and the lesser development of information about associations and memory, experimental psychology, in its first fifty years, produced scientific information of a reasonably high order.

At the same time, some other people were studying animal behavior. The historical context of this activity and the reasons for its development are not quite so easy to explain. The experimental study of animal behavior largely grew out of the Darwinian natural selection theory of evolution. Naturalists after Darwin published lengthy accounts, based on anecdotal evidence, of how natural selection affected animal behavior. These accounts, sometimes coming from the fanciful tales of travelers, excited the skepticism of scientists with a laboratory bent. Some investigators took it on themselves to study the capacities of animals in the laboratory both as a way of countering the fanciful tales and as a means of studying adaptation. Using in part the newly developed techniques of experimental psychology, students in Germany and the United States tested the capacity of various animals to react to different stimuli.

The experimental study of animal behavior thus came into psychology in a rather indirect way. But in the decade that followed its introduction, it assumed central importance. It did so because of the convergence of a number of events. One was the appearance of the experiments and points of view of the Russian physiologist Ivan P. Pavlov. Pavlov's work, largely concerned with conditioned reflexes, came to the attention of psychologists at a time when there was a movement within American psychology to convert psychology into a physiologically based science. This attempt was in no small measure the single-handed result of the efforts of John B. Watson, the initiator of the behavioristic movement. Although he was trained as an experimental psychologist, Watson came under the influence of Jacques Loeb and H. H. Donaldson, who were biologists on the faculty at the University of Chicago while he was a graduate student there. Loeb espoused an extreme mechanistic view concerning the mental capacities of animals. According to Loeb, animals were machines, and Watson came to assume that man was basically such a machine, differing from simpler animals only in complexity of construction.

Watson, both in his scientific work and in his polemic writings, erased much of the barrier that existed between classical experimental psychology and experimentation with animals. He did so by denying that it was consciousness that early experimental psychologists studied and insisting that, at bottom, they were studying the same kinds of things that the experimental students of animal behavior studied, namely the responses of organisms. To Watson it was a matter of minor detail that the responses of human beings were largely verbal. Most aspects of Watson's experimental work are now neglected, but his doctrine of behaviorism has had an enormous influence on psychology and related fields. Evidence of Watson's intellectual influence is the commonly accepted term "behavioral sciences" and the fact that *Time* magazine now carries a section labeled simply "Behavior."

Watson's work took place just before the First World War. As the academic world and psychology in particular emerged from that war, the opportunities for the new point of view in psychology were many. The academic world in general and psychology in particular experienced discontinuity. The dominance of the German universities was disrupted, and the views held by the conservative, German-trained academicians in American universities disappeared. The change was a permanent one. American psychology even today, in its theoretical state, is still largely dominated by the trilogy of behaviorism, operationalism, and logical positivism. Logical positivism, the view that science is concerned only with empirical knowledge, was a development of Central Europe and came to the United States in the 1920s and especially with the European refugees of the 1930s. Its antimetaphysical views and its idolatrous attitude toward the physical sciences made it a natural ally of operationalism and behaviorism in American psychology. The association of these points of view is not a necessary one, although it certainly is a real one. They all fitted together to produce the ideal of experimental psychology that has served two or more generations of American psychologists.

Experimental psychology, purged of the notion that it studied consciousness, began to emphasize control of behavior and made the animal experiment, rather than the classical introspective report, the central theoretical interest. Behaviorism, with its emphasis on stimuli and responses to stimuli and (at least in its early stages) its development of and reliance on the reflex as explanation, provided the main theoretical theme. Logical positivism, with its insistence that only statements capable of verification are meaningful, and operationalism, with its insistence on making concrete concepts out of those that were abstract, provided the methodological themes.

After the First World War, psychologists talked less and less about conscious experience. Textbooks no longer described psychology as the study of consciousness, but began to describe it as the study of behavior. Because this was also the time during which Freud's ideas were coming into psychology, psychology textbooks were often schizophrenic, talking about behavior on the one hand and unconscious processes (which imply, of course, conscious ones) on the other. The dominant theoretical direction, however, was provided by the experimental researchers. These researchers, following Watson, argued that the goal of scientific psychology was the prediction and control of behavior, and the way to control behavior was to control stimuli.

Stimulus-response psychology

This, in the briefest form, was the message of the behavioristic theories of psychology from the thirties up to the present time. The important theories of this era were nearly all stimulus-response theories. But because it is not possible to specify direct stimulus-response relationships for any interesting range of phenomena, behavioral theorists found it necessary to invent concepts with a rather curious status, which required some methodological explanation. There was, for example, in one well-known theory[3] a concept known as "habit strength." This concept referred neither to the stimulus conditions that controlled the behavior of organisms nor to behavior itself, but rather to some hypothesized internal state of the organism through which the effects of successive experiences were added. Habit strength was a theoretical variable, or hypothetical construct, as such notions came to be called under the influence of the logical positivists. Some psychologists preferred to call a concept like habit strength an *intervening variable*.[4]

The more highly developed theories produced mathematically precise statements of the relation among stimuli (external controlled conditions), responses, and hypothetical states, or intervening variables. Psychologists thought of conditions internal to the responding organism as intervening variables because they intervened between stimuli and responses in some temporal and causative sense. Intervening variables were often, however, familiar notions from everyday psychology—habit, attention, expectation. Some behavioristic theories did, then, contain propositions that could be said to be part of a theory of mind. But the kind of mind that these propositions produced was a strange one. It was one in which nearly all the important processes depended on elementary and direct relations between input and output. Some of the variables

[3] C. L. Hull, *Principles of Behavior* (New York: Appleton-Century-Crofts, 1943).

[4] The term "intervening variable" was invented by the influential theoretical psychologist Edward C. Tolman. Tolman used the term to express the idea that theoretical constructs in psychology intervened between the stimulus and the response.

of the laboratory research generated out of such a theory were the intensity of stimulation, the number of times a particular act had been rewarded (or reinforced), the delay between response and reinforcement, and the intensity of drive (which was often interpreted as intensity of a particular kind of stimulation). These theoretical constructs (or intervening variables) and the relations among them were modeled on simple observations. The relations between a simple stimulus and response in a reflex (or habit) were supposed to be mediated by events that did not differ in principle from what could be observed—that is, they were simply small-scale reflexes internal to (or in between) the observable stimulus and response. The internal or hypothetical reflexes were supposed to happen in between the observable stimulus and response.

The nature of the independent variables and their relation to the experimental method generally were of crucial importance in these stimulus-response theories. The heart of the experimental method, as mentioned earlier, lies in the ability of the investigator to control some condition (independent variable) upon which some other condition (dependent variable) is said to be contingent. A change in the independent variable should be reflected in a change in the dependent variable if a contingency holds. And if the experimental method is to be useful, the link of control over the independent variable must be simple and direct. The experimenter must be certain that if the proper apparatus is activated, the independent variable changes in a particular way. If the independent variable is the intensity of a pure tone, for example, there should be no doubt that when the experimenter turns up the amplifier, the power of the sound at the ear of an experimental subject increases. An experimenter must be satisfied with the assumed link between his "operations" and the stimulus delivered to the subject before he can begin work, and if he suspects trouble he has a technician check his apparatus. It is equally important that the link between the independent and the dependent variable be simple and direct; there must be no loose linkage. This aspect of experimentation is often forgotten. If one is to apply the experimental method to the investigation of a theory in which a whole complicated pattern of intervening concepts comes between the stimulus (independent variable) and the response (dependent variable), the theory must be one for which something other than guessing and surmising provide the evidence.

In psychological theory there is no established way of specifying all the subtle and intricate links that are said to exist between independent and dependent variables. Psychological theories are often primitive and thus sometimes not very useful. In various branches of the physical sciences a complicated theoretical network usually intervenes between an event controlled by the investigator and an observation, but all except a small and rationally controllable bit of the theory has been well worked out and empirically verified in advance of any particular observation. The whole of modern atomic theory, for example, may intervene between a physicist's throwing a switch in a particular piece of apparatus and the effect recorded on a photographic plate a few moments later. The physicist, however, has little doubt that he can give an account of all the things that happen as a consequence of his switch being thrown, an account derived from three centuries of the interplay of theory with experiment. If he has doubts, a major revolution in physics takes place. Thus, even though an indirect relation between the independent and the dependent variables must be the case in experiments in the physical sciences as well as in the psychological sciences, the extent to which that network can be specified differs among the various sciences.

The traditional physical sciences—chemistry and physics—are preeminent in experimentation because experimentation is based on a developed theory, not the other way around. Psychological experimentation often fails, not through failure in the experimental method itself, but because theory that is supposed to mediate the events under consideration is not sufficiently detailed to make any single psychological experiment easily interpreted. No series of experiments or no experimental science itself should be given the task of testing a very large and poorly specified series of intervening links such as those provided by the psychological theories of the past generations. The successful application of the experimental method to the examination of psychological theory demands that the investigator know what he is doing. In the rush to generalize the application of the experimental method, psychologists often forget this. The result is that psychological experiments are sometimes what Wilhelm Wundt called in another context "pretend experiments." Such experiments depend as often on self-deception on the part of the experimenter as on the apparatus of experimental theory. The interpretation of any particular outcome depends as much on preconception as on the results.

The current state

This, then, is the current state of much of the application of the scientific method in basic problems in psychology. It is compounded of (1) the classical commitment of psychology to experimentation on the model of nineteenth-century physics, (2) the skepticism of the antitheological movement among the heirs to Scottish faculty psychology in the United States and England, (3) the biologically based behavioristic revolution, (4) the antimetaphysical epistemology of logical positivism, and (5) the pragmatic laboratory-oriented methodological strictures of operationalism. Each of these influences has served a useful function in the history of modern psychology. Wundt's great discovery, experimental psychology, a discovery furthered by the investigation of higher mental processes by Hermann v. Ebbinghaus, showed that some problems in the study of the human mind could be subjected to laboratory experimentation. The antitheological skepticism of late nineteenth-century American and English psychology served as a broad base from which to develop the objective consideration of questions about man and his place in nature. This consideration was consistent with, and derived in part from, the biological revolution represented by Darwinian theory. The behavioristic revolution in turn served to broaden the base of the original German experimental psychology. It questioned the reliance of a psychology based on the limited methods of introspection, and it showed that aspects of the human mind and human behavior rejected by Wundt and his students as beyond science could be studied by objective methods. Finally, logical positivism and its philosophically less highly developed sister, operationalism, cleared away some lingering questions about the metaphysical status of mind. The philosophy of science of the early twentieth century asked psychology to purge itself of questions to which no solution could be found through the ordinary methods of science.

The fate of revolutions is that some outworn orthodoxy becomes replaced by a new one that very quickly also begins to show signs of wear. The lines of opinion harden and the new dogma becomes as rigid as the old. For example, many contemporary psychologists view with moral indignation the idea that any considerable portion of the nature of man's thinking processes could be innate, as some would argue today. But this kind of rigidity is as restrictive as the reactions of the moral philosophers of the Scottish school to notions about evolution. Even the dogma that one must ask only questions that can be answered by reference to accepted scientific procedures and operations, a dogma derived from logical positivism and operationalism, can soon harden into the rejection of anything new. The only operations appropriate to psychological science become those of the laboratory. The things that can be done in the laboratory together with the characterization of these in quasi-mathematical terms as independent and dependent variables become the goal of all psychological research and the sole arbiter of psychological theory. New methods and new problems are greeted with hostility. These kinds of restrictions on psychology have proved to be inhibiting to the development and acceptance of new ideas.

A few years ago some linguists [5] demonstrated to psychologists that one could answer penetrating psychological questions about the nature of human language without experimentation or even the explicit collection of data in the statistical tradition of psychology. The initial reaction of many experimental psychologists was to say that what these linguists were doing was not science. It was not science because it could not be found in the laboratory and it did not seem to lead to the laboratory. It was not science because there was nothing to which one could apply statistics. Linguists showed, for example, that some important theories on the way in which people generated sentences could be ruled out simply by virtue of the fact that there are, in many languages of the world,

---

[5] The influence of linguistics on psychology has come particularly from the work of N. Chomsky and his associates. See N. Chomsky, *Language and Mind* (New York: Harcourt, Brace & Jovanovich, 1968).

what linguists call "discontinuous constituents." These are constructions in which two parts of a phrase or some other linguistic element are separated by intervening constructions. There is, in general, no limit to the number of constructions that may intervene. The existence of discontinuous constituents in the very general case, coupled with certain fundamental facts about language (such as that no rules govern the length of sentences), rules out some very powerful, explicit theories on how human beings might generate sentences. These theories were important to psychologists because they were very close to those that had been dominant in the psychology of language and verbal learning for a generation. Most psychologists have been taught to assume that experimentation and "evidence" of a statistically reliable and acceptable nature should be the sole criteria for the elimination of theories. They are not accustomed to the possibility that showing the existence of a possible mode of thinking or behavior or a possible linguistic construction could in itself be of enormous theoretical importance. Some facts about human behavior and thinking are so obvious that they scarcely need a laboratory experiment to demonstrate them, and they may be far more important than the facts that come out of the laboratory.

As with the questioning of all established dogma, even dogma in science, criticism generates controversy. The critical reaction to the established position often comes at a time when it is celebrating its greatest triumphs. This is true of experimental psychology. The past fifteen years have seen the expansion of classical experimental psychology—the study of sensory, perceptual, and certain simple motor and cognitive functions—into areas that were supposed to be immune to experimental study. Social psychology, developmental psychology, and the study of personality are now said to be experimental. It is argued that because social and developmental psychologists investigate natural events too, it should be possible to apply the methods of scientific study to these areas. Hence, the experimental paradigm of late nineteenth-century science has been extended to fields in psychology that are closer to the traditional interests of humanists. That these areas provide networks of established fact and conception that are even less well articulated than the traditional areas of psychology has not hindered this development. Many textbooks in child psychology and social psychology present passionate propaganda on behalf of the experimental movement in the study of social psychology, psychological development, and personality. The past few years have also seen the establishment of a series of new journals called *Experimental Child Psychology, Experimental Social Psychology,* and so on.

If we examine the effects of this application of the experimental method to what is sometimes called the softer side of psychology, we can see some of the worst consequences of the whole development of this traditional view of psychological method. One reason so much current empirical research is trivial and pointless is that the experimental method is inapplicable to many problems in social psychology and the psychology of personality. The problems contemporary social psychologists choose to study are usually not trivial, but the methods by which these problems are investigated often reduce the problems to triviality. For example, one profoundly significant issue investigated by many contemporary social psychologists is the extent to which adult human beings may adhere to some commonly accepted aspects of the moral code in the absence of external surveillance. An experimental social psychologist may investigate this problem by inventing a social situation in which the subject is deceived into believing that it might be possible for him to steal or acquire by morally unacceptable means some trifling sum of money. The behavior of subjects in this situation, under the influence of various conditions, is the object of experimental study. But the investigator seldom limits the results of such experiments to the situations studied. Since it would be only of trivial importance to know that people having certain demographic or socioeconomic characteristics do or do not steal five dollars under certain circumstances, the investigator usually intends that the situation he uses in his laboratory stand for a whole host of situations that are similar in vague and unspecified ways. Only his intuition guides him, for he gives no rigorous criteria for determining which situations resemble the experimental test and which do not.

Thus, there is no way of knowing precisely how to generalize the results found in a particular testing situation. The testing situation may be placed under even greater strain by the introduction of some experimental operation, such as the presence of a confederate of the experimenter. The confederate may attempt to persuade the subject one way or the other. The confederate's presence and arguments constitute a state of an "independent variable" in the experiment. These experimental operations are presumed to control what the subject thinks and does. But such control is only on the naive faith of the experimenter. The experimenter does not know what goes on in the subject's mind. In all such experiments in which the subject is supposedly the "stooge" of a confederate of the experimenter (and these are common in contemporary social psychology), the experimenter implicitly assumes that the subject believes that the other person in the experiment is *not* a confederate of the experimenter. In fact, it is usually essential that the subject not believe himself to be in an experiment at all, or at least not in an experiment in social psychology. But belief is a complicated state, as even psychologists know, and it cannot simply be dismissed by asserting that a subject believes or does not believe, or is deluded or not deluded, or is deluded partly or not deluded partly. Beliefs are sometimes clear and well formed while at other times they are inchoate and almost impossible to state without being changed in the process of being stated. A subject may have to invent all sorts of myths, stories, or hypotheses to account for the remarkable series of events he faces in the psychological laboratory. These hypotheses may bear no relation to what the experimenter thinks is going on in the subject's mind. But they may have some relevance to what a subject does in the experimental situation. Usually, in such experiments, the investigator makes only a feeble attempt to find out what the subject's beliefs and hypotheses might be. In short, the subject does not always have in his head the conceptions that the experimenter thinks he has, yet the interpretation of such experiments often depends on that assumption.

Finally, the generalization of the results of these experiments depends on what would be regarded in certain other branches of psychology as incredibly naive assumptions about the generality of traits in people. For example, many recent experiments have been concerned with the extent to which people are willing to engage in altruistic actions. Altruism could be indicated by the willingness of a subject (again, in a deception experiment) to come to the aid of the experimenter's confederate, who feigns distress. Suppose that the experiment is a success—that is to say, the subject's beliefs about the experimental situation are those that the experimenter wants him to have: he truly believes that someone is in distress. We are then asked, on the basis of his being willing to put himself out a little while waiting for an appointment in the psychological laboratory (the appointment is often the cover story used to lure the subject into the laboratory), to believe that this situation taps some unitary and invariant trait of altruism. In the interpretation placed on such experiments by social psychologists, altruism often appears to be a state independent of time and circumstance, subject only to the external controls invented by the experimenter.

Not all experimental social psychologists who work with these subtle problems are as insensitive to their difficulties as the above discussion suggests. Many experimenters follow procedures that do in fact provide a mine of information in experimental situations of this sort, and such experimenters are cautious and skeptical about the kinds of inferences that may be derived from their data. But the reader of recent empirical literature in social psychology should examine with great care and reserved opinion the ostensible conclusions of experiments having to do with such important matters as altruism, social morality, social guilt, and other matters of human significance. This is particularly the case when it appears that a conclusion about these matters is derived purely on the basis of empirical evidence.

There are some problems in psychology for which the precise and powerful tools of the classical experimental model developed in the physical sciences from the seventeenth through the nineteenth century are preeminently successful. The study of sensory functions and, to a certain extent, the study of perceptual abilities are examples. So when it is said that the experimental method, its associated behavioristic theory, and reliance on a particular philosophy of science have reached the limits of their influence, the statement is only partly valid. A scientist with the problem of correlating the discrimination of color with functions of the receptors in the human eye can produce a scientific triumph by the rigorous application of the classical methods. In fact, many of the truly significant advances in certain traditional areas of experimental psychology are the result of the refinement of long-available techniques. New developments in psychological measurement, such as signal detection theory, coupled with new methods in physical and biological assay, as in microspectographic analysis, can produce new and powerful conceptions about the nature of human color vision. Furthermore, certain problems in social psychology do lend themselves to study through the application of the experimental method. But the attempt to press the whole traditional scientific apparatus into developing areas in psychology induces the very discrepancy between the significance of psychology and the triviality of the problems actually investigated that alarms and distresses student and psychologist alike.

Psychological research faces a future of increasing diversity. The techniques that were at one time so confidently assumed to apply to all of psychology do not. Certain techniques are inapplicable to certain problems, and, furthermore, because some methods cannot be applied, the kinds of inferences one may derive from observations in certain fields of psychology must be limited in a fundamental way. The rest of this book is given over to a discussion of the kinds of things we can sensibly do with various psychological techniques of investigation and the kinds of conclusions we can arrive at from the application of those techniques. We shall discover that the line between conclusions and theories that are "scientific" and those that are mythical or fanciful is not nearly so sharp as we may have been led to suppose. We shall also discover that the very substance—the abstract nature—of psychological theories changes in radical ways as we move from one area of psychology to another. What works with one problem will not work with another.

2
PSYCHOLOGICAL
THEORY

Around the beginning of the twentieth century, when it seemed apparent that the important advances in knowledge in the future would be scientific ones, a group of philosophers turned from the general study of human knowledge, or epistemology, to the particular study of the nature of scientific knowledge. At that time the great epistemological debate between the tradition of British empiricism, represented best by Hume, and German idealism, exemplified by Kant, had about run its course. Philosophers of the new century turned from traditional questions to the development of logic in the image of mathematics and the application of that logic to science. One of the results of this movement was the dramatic growth of interest in the philosophy of science.

Early efforts in the philosophy of science in this century created an idealized picture, in the image of physics, of what scientists did, by stating a theory of scientific activity. Despite the fact that the original model was physics, that idealization has had a significant effect on psychology in particular and on the social sciences in general. Social scientists—probably as a result of the vagueness and uncertainty associated with their subject matter—have always felt constrained to live up to the ideal, or at least to discuss it at interminable length.

The philosophy of science, particularly as interpreted by behavioral and social scientists, has always had a prescriptive air about it. Psychologists who interpret the philosophers of science are really telling us what to do when they give us a description of

28

the nature of scientific theory. The fact that their ideal picture of science is hardly ever realized even in the most highly developed of the classical physical sciences, such as mechanics, and certainly never in psychology, has not discouraged people from insisting that psychology must live by the rules of scientific investigation formalized by early twentieth-century philosophers of science. Idealizations are useful kinds of abstractions to have around, for they tell us that to which we shall aspire. The crisis in psychology today, however, is largely a product of the still current idealization of science.

Scientific theories in psychology

A scientific theory is a set of propositions or statements, some of which are axioms and some of which are assumptions. It is distinguished from pure mathematics or logic by the fact that some propositions can be coordinated with empirical data to produce facts. The axioms are fundamental definitions that cannot be either proved or demonstrated. The assumptions state hypotheses about events in the world. Through the application of some logical calculus, these propositions or statements lead to *theorems*. Theorems are statements that can be regarded as logical consequences of assumptions and axioms. Some of the theorems in a scientific theory (as opposed to those in pure mathematics) make statements about events in the real world. These are the statements coordinated with the results of empirical research. Ideally, the measurements obtained from research can be placed on a one-to-one relationship with some of the theorems. If the empirical facts and the theorems agree, the theory is said to be a good one.

Almost nothing, even in the most highly developed physical sciences, even approaches such an idealized account. Some of the physical sciences depend on mathematics to make them more like this picture. Even though few aspects of science actually conform to this image, it is useful, particularly to those branches of science in which conceptual abstractions are common. This is the case in physics, some aspects of linguistics, and some social sciences, such as economics.

Theories can be regarded as powerful tools for examining the implications of assumptions about the world. The most highly developed theories make their assumptions explicit, but in less formally developed theories assumptions are often hidden or simply implied by some other aspect of the theory. Even when theories are explicit, their "practical" or "experimental" implications are often arrived at by metaphoric argument rather than by rigorous mathematic or logical derivation. Logicians and others sometimes argue that all theories should be explicit. They say that informal theories are always imprecisely stated and lead to scientific errors. The assumptions behind them are not ever made clear, and their implications are not logically derived.

Something like a formal theory appears in a limited way in psychology. Some parts of the theory of learning and conditioning have been formalized in ways deliberately modeled on the ideals set by the philosophy of science. Various other problems, such as those involving decision processes and psychophysical processes, have been examined through the application of precise and sophisticated theories. But to most psychologists, the attempts to widen the scope of mathematical psychology (as much of the rigorous theorizing in psychology has come to be called) appear not to be very fruitful, given the intellectual effort necessary. These attempts seem to be sterile because they generate only a few theorems, which have to do with matters of little general significance so far as the larger problems of psychology are concerned. Investigators sometimes invent assumptions not so much because they are important to the psychological process as because they are easy to work with mathematically. Some psychologists have always maintained that mathematical learning theorists search where the lamp post is rather than where the coin was lost. In any event, the application of a highly formal and explicit theory has not been of central importance in most of those areas of psychology that people other than experimental psychologists think are important.

In the technical sense meant by philosophers of science, there is very little that can be called theory in psychology. Those theories that have been rigorous enough to meet high standards have been attacked as being sterile. There is a question as to whether such sterility is supposed to be the result of the application of highly developed and rigorous techniques, as some critics claim, or of the application of an erroneous or misguided theory derived from classical associationism, stimulus-response psychology, and Pavlovian conditioning. There is no necessary connection between stimulus-response theory and highly developed mathematical theorizing—as indeed the development of certain aspects of psychological measurement and modern psycholinguistics show us—but for historical reasons, many psychologists associate substantive mathematical theories in psychology with the stimulus-response tradition.

Why some theories
are better than others

Most psychological theories fail to approach the ideals set for them by the philosophy of science in respect to correctness, or truth value. Many concerned laymen and not a few scientists take the view that the whole purpose of science is to search for truth. These same people often think that the truth consists of a set of propositions that remain unchallenged forever, once properly established. The truth is the truth. But at the same time everyone knows that scientific theories change. In fact, the history of any particular science shows that there is almost nothing that remains an eternal verity. A few very general empirical principles, such as those discovered by Archimedes, have lasted a long time. But even these, when incorporated into scientific theory, are part of larger bodies of propositions that change from time to time. In short, the whole structure of scientific truth changes.

The early twentieth-century philosophers of science agreed that there is no means of finding out whether or not a scientific theory is true forever. Nor can the truth or falsity of a scientific theory, in the ordinary course of things, be decided by a single critical test. One can only decide that, given the circumstances at the moment, one theory is in some way better than another. Philosophers of science have argued endlessly about the possibility of applying critical tests to find out which among competing scientific theories is the best. Critical tests should be provided by theorems that differentiate one set of scientific propositions from another in some definitive way. An example sometimes singled out is the comparison of various theories concerning space-time transformations within classical Newtonian theory by means of an examination of the earth's velocity with respect to some fixed reference. Older theories asserted that the velocity must be determinable, while the newer, relativistic theories assert that it need not be. Even granting the example, it is seldom in any but the most highly developed scientific theory that a single theorem or observation will serve to choose between two alternative scientific theories. Experimental psychologists of the past generation spent a good bit of time, largely in vain, searching for critical tests of one or another theory of learning.

At its best, a critical test can only tell us that one theory—for the moment—is to be preferred. It cannot tell us that one particular theory is true for all eternity. We arc deprived of the comfort of any absolute truth in science, for the strongest test of a scientific theory is only a comparative one.

The actual situation is even less ideal from the standpoint of the old notion that science should be the search for truth. Most theories generate some propositions that do not seem to be in accordance with empirical facts. Most theories contain "approximations." For this reason they inevitably fail to show a precise one-to-one correspondence with empirical facts. For example, the experimental investigation of many mathematical theories of learning demands the assumption that all individuals are in principle alike and differ only in a random way. This is an oversimplification deliberately built into the theories in order to make the mathematics less complicated. Other theories make incorrect predictions of experimental observations. The authors of such theories may attempt to repair them by some *ad hoc* additions. These factors may prevent a sharp and clear choice between theories. A few classical cases provide examples for philosophers of science, but even those leave doubts.

One theory dominates over others because it works, or is fashionable, or is esthetically pleasing. In short, scientific theories survive for a variety of reasons, some of them not very intellectual, much less centered around some criterion of truth. Some advantages of particular theories can hardly even be stated. These advantages often have to do not with abstract philosophical questions but with questions of what could better be described as the sociology of science.

The whole matter is often rendered even more mysterious by the fact that there is not always a rivalry between two theories, one of which is supposed to be better than another. The comparison is often between one theory and no theory at all, between the best thing that someone can think of at the moment and nothing. Therefore, some scientists—and certainly some psychologists— elect to suspend judgment about the truth of a theory. These scientists are often in a peculiar position because they subscribe to the general point of view summarized by twentieth-century philosophy of science. They regard the development of scientific theories as the ultimate goal of all scientific activities. They may say, however, that the field in which they are working is not sufficiently developed at the present time to warrant the elaboration of theories. In psychology, some of the behaviorists, particularly those associated with the point of view of B. F. Skinner,[1] have adopted this attitude toward psychological theory.

Occasionally, the comparison may be among a multitude of theories, no one of which has sufficiently strong empirical validity to make a good case for itself. Often these theories differ from one another in a number of small but bewildering ways. Thus, in the heyday of learning theories, there wasn't one "behavioral theory" opposed by, say, one "cognitive" theory, but a whole bundle of theories on each side. This situation characterizes the chaos of much of psychology, but it is also surprisingly characteristic of aspects of many other sciences, including some branches of the physical sciences.

In the ideal case, one theory is preferred over another because it can describe or generate more facts that turn out to be empirically sound, because it is formally complete and parsimonious, or

[1] B. F. Skinner, *Cumulative Record* (New York: Appleton-Century-Crofts, 1959).

because it may be easily incorporated into some larger set of propositions. But the real world is less orderly, and psychological theories are as much at the mercy of current fashion as the facts they produce. The facts used to establish the empirical plausibility of a given theory may be trivial and unrelated to the interests of anyone other than the investigator who is testing the theory. There is no way to establish in any rigorous and formal way the centrality or significance of one set of facts over another, and as the interests and attitudes of psychologists change, the significance may shift from one set of facts to another. At one time, in the study of verbal behavior, the rate at which people learned various combinations of nonsense syllables provided the facts of greatest central interest to theorists. More recently, the facts that interest theorists center around the ability of people to remember and paraphrase ordinary sentences. The shift in emphasis to different kinds of facts makes different kinds of theories fashionable. For example, theories about the serial position curve in nonsense syllable learning are no longer popular, while theories about sentence processing now enjoy a certain vogue.

Theories in historical perspective

There is a doctrine to the effect that all sciences in their early stages are empirical and qualitative. Later, they become quantitative and theoretical. In fact, however, different sciences have developed in different ways. Much of classical physics grew out of various technologies, many of which were quite old and were often combined with magical or religious features. For example, priests in ancient Egypt were able to predict the rise and fall of the Nile. These predictions depended on the development of a prescientific technology that was partly astronomical in character. That information was part of the esoteric or hermetic knowledge of the priesthood. Yet it, or something very like it, provided the groundwork for the rational prescientific work of the Greek philosophers. The origins of nearly all ancient science and mathematics were closely identified with religion and magic. It took Greek rationalism to begin to make the break between magic and science. Even so, scientists have continued to be associated or identified with the priestly castes. Some of the current myths about science may derive from that association.

Some sciences, of course, came into existence without the association of technology, magic, and religion. Modern biology, particularly taxonomic biology and the theory of evolution, grew out of the prescientific theories of the organization of nature. Other aspects of biology came from medicine and the empirical application of herbs and other agents in the treatment of disease. Psychology and the social sciences have even more complicated origins, partly because they depend on the development of earlier sciences and also because they themselves came into existence during an era in which there was a self-conscious concern with the development of science.

Scientific psychology came into existence, almost as Athena, fullblown. It was born in an age when people had come to realize that there was something called *science* and that it had a special status in human affairs and knowledge. It was largely a product of the movement toward specialization in the German academic world. The idea of separate and independent scientific disciplines is an invention of the German universities of the nineteenth century.[2] It has reached new heights of development in the direct descendant of those German universities, American graduate schools. The idea that some scientists are physicists and some, chemists, while others are geologists and zoologists, is primarily a German idea. It was not always so. In nineteenth-century England, physicists were often identified simply as natural philosophers, and biologists, as evidenced by the well-known examples of Charles Darwin and his half-cousin, Sir Francis Galton, were often simply gifted amateurs. But the German idea of a scientific profession has been universally accepted in this century. Thus, the development of scientific psychology, though complicated and dependent on the growth of other intellectual disciplines, has an independent institutional character. Partly because of its formal origins in nineteenth-century Germany, psychology developed a

[2] The German universities had been revolutionized in the period following the Napoleonic wars. An important part of that revolution was the vastly enhanced status accorded the developing physical sciences.

peculiar self-conscious concern with the nature of knowledge, especially scientific knowledge, and with the organization of intellectual disciplines.

Thus, the idea that all sciences start out in some empirical prescientific state intermingled with magic and are developed to some theoretical, scientifically respectable state independent of magic is an oversimplification. Each science has a history of its own, determined by the context of human institutions in which each is embedded. Nearly all sciences are mixtures of the formal and the informal, of the empirical and the theoretical, of the old and the new, of the traditional and the revolutionary. The classical physical sciences are more nearly committed to a complete formalization than the other sciences, but that commitment is only a matter of degree.

The complex structure of the various sciences guarantees that no scientific theory can be examined by any single, general criterion. The most significant psychological theories are never really made to meet the difficult criteria demanded of them by philosophers of science. That is because these theories were not *designed* by philosophers of science. They grew out of the matrix of problems that defines modern scientific psychology. Some of these problems originated in physical science and for a while were distinguishable from physical problems only by a kind of epistemological argument. A good example is the theory of color advanced by Isaac Newton near the end of the seventeenth century. It was partly a psychological theory and partly a physical theory designed to account, among other things, for how spectral colors mixed. Not until well into the nineteenth century was it possible to sort out the psychological from the physical in the theory of color. By that time well-developed theories about the physiological processes in the eye responsible for color were available. Because of this history and because of the subject matter, the development of even that part of Newtonian color theory that is psychological— and is still being developed in empirical and theoretical form— conforms more to the standards of the model set by physics than do other aspects of psychology.

For another example of the origin of theoretical problems in psychology, we might turn to the question of how people change psychologically as they get older. Does the development of children recapitulate phylogeny, as the early American psychologist G. Stanley Hall said it did? Hall argued that individual human beings traced the history of the race. They were premammal fetuses, complete with gill slits, became primates in babyhood, savages as children, and civilized human beings only as adults. This notion implies an intuitive theory of development, based on analogies from biology, that in method, content, and structure is light-years away from a theory of color vision. Modern theories of psychological development are still modeled on the biological notions of growth and maturity.

Psychological theories, hypotheses, and facts are a jumble of notions. Thus, it is difficult to say what single purpose psychological theory serves. The strict criteria set for psychological theory by philosophers of science will apply only in some cases, which have thus far proven to be samewhat disappointing. These cases are some highly developed mathematical theories in psychology, but their content has never attracted much general interest outside of psychology. The best applications of mathematics in psychology appear to be not in theory but in the development of such methods as psychological scaling and measurement, although developments in decision theory and related topics provide exceptions.

Theory and myth

Psychological theories have a variety of uses, some of which serve the needs associated with myth or mythical explanation. The epistemological value of myths is low. They are not designed for knowledge; myths are designed for comfort and for emotional and esthetic satisfaction. Although it is a cynic's view to say that all psychological theory is but myth, the line between theory and myth is not a sharp one. Some psychological theories, even some that are formal and explicit, must be regarded primarily as myths because they make explicit contact with the world only in some single fact that they are supposed to explain. Even the highly formal mathematical theories of learning of a generation ago fitted this description. They argued about hypothetical nerve networks in the brain. But since there was no way of knowing about such networks or of testing the consequences of supposing their existence, they could be regarded only as highly developed and elaborate myths.

The distinction between myth and theory, then, is not simply one of explicitness and rigor. Myths may be just as formal and well-developed as scientific theory. The difference between scientific theory and myth is the extent to which the assertions in them try to provide a detailed articulation with reality. Myths sometimes do make assertions about external reality. In fact, the myths with which most of us are familiar nearly all do. They tell us how the sky got to be the way it is, or how fire was brought to earth, or how the sea became salty. But these myths account for things by a number of assumptions, most of which have little or no credibility and largely depend on totally mysterious superhuman action. Thus, only one "test"—the event for which the myth is supposed to account—is used to justify a large number of strange and implausible events. The existence of mythical beings, of someone called Prometheus, of the Titans, and of an incredible salt mill are not meant to be realistic assumptions, but fanciful ones. The chief contact with reality in a myth may be only in the ultimate point of the myth.

This is the respect in which useful scientific theories differ from myths. The assumptions of scientific theory are not meant to be fanciful, or incredible, or to lack contact with other aspects of reality or science. They are meant to be themselves part of a larger framework of human knowledge that occupies an orderly place in the intellectual world. Furthermore, scientific theories do not seek to explain just a single fact in the world (that the sea is salty, for example) but a whole range of facts. Thus, although there is a resemblance in some respects, scientific theories in the best sense are not myths, for their very structures differ.

Some ideas incorporated as parts of science are indeed myths. A great deal of classical psychoanalysis is stated in the framework of myth. It has exploratory power of a sort, but it is no accident that the theory itself is described in the language of myth and ancient drama. Its truths are to be found as much in the empathic response it brings forth as in the realities of human nature with which it deals.

Metaphors and models
in psychological theories

Psychological theories can have implications beyond those usually assumed to be valid by the tradition of positivism in science. These implications are apparent in various *metaphors* of description. It is sometimes said, for example, that theories are road maps to natural phenomena. Another metaphor says that theories provide rational cookbooks for the discovery of new facts. Even more common is the assertion that theories provide *models* of important natural events. Each one of these metaphorical descriptions of the nature of theory implies some function of theorizing beyond those implied by formal philosophers of science. They all imply that a theory is something more than an intellectual exercise in generating propositions equally useful to a human being or computer. They all imply that theories have peculiar and intrinsic value to human beings.

Theories, like myths, often provide simplified descriptions in a way suited to human understanding. Such use of theory has particular appeal in the social sciences. Physical theories can exist as kinds of abstractions in their own right. Maxwell's equations have a kind of austere beauty about them that derives partly from their purely formal characteristics and partly from the remarkable natural phenomena they serve to explain. Many of us also like models, however, and we particularly like models that we can visualize. Thus, the Rutherford-Bohr model of the atom is still of some intrinsic interest to amateur scientists, but except among historians of science is of no great urgency to physicists and chemists. On the other hand, intuitively satisfying models of social and personal interaction are of fundamental interest to nearly everyone, and they will still be of interest to most of us even when, for more scientific purposes, they have been supplanted by more abstract notions.

Not everyone realizes the extent to which particular theories in the social sciences are cast in the form of models or metaphorical representations of various aspects of reality familiar to us. Psychoanalytic theory has already been mentioned in this respect. Two essential features of psychoanalytic theory are cast in the metaphor of the drama. In one of these, there is an internal conflict between the ego and the id, and in the other there is an external conflict between the individual and his social world (particularly his family). The idea of human personality development as a drama—with separate but interdependent acts, as in any drama—is implicit in classical psychoanalytic theory. It provides one of the reasons for the enormous appeal of psychoanalytic theory. The popular appeal of psychoanalytic theory has been as important as its explanatory value.

Models and metaphors serve no absolutely necessary scientific function, although they do have direct and indirect pragmatic uses. And it should be remembered that all descriptions of a metaphorical sort oversimplify. This is so because behind the proposition "X is like Y" is always the qualification that X resembles Y with respect to conditions A and B but not with respect to C. Thus, human life is like a stage drama in some respects, but not in others. The atom in the Rutherford-Bohr model is like a solar system in some respects, but not in others. Scale models share this property. A miniature model of a river constructed by a geologist is like the real river in as many respects as possible, but it will surely differ from the real river, if nothing else, in scale factor. Scale factors turn out to have important physical characteristics that must be taken into account in any information derived from a physical model.[3]

The purpose of the model and the metaphor is to state the essence of something without the encumbrance of all the irrelevant or minor details that make understanding difficult. In models, as in all metaphors, the description is somewhat inaccurate. But we are

[3] Scale is especially important in biological matters. A grasp of its role in growth can come from a reading of the now famous classic, D'Arcy Thompson, *On Growth and Form*, 2nd ed. (London: Cambridge University Press, 1942).

willing to accept the inaccuracy because our minds cannot grasp all the detail. We are free, of course, to reject what is inaccurate in the comparison.

Formalists in the philosophy of science do not like models and they like metaphor even less.[4] Models and metaphors serve no logical function. Purists dislike models simply because, in principle, any consequence of a model can be stated *without* a model. In other words, the logical propositions that are represented by the model can all be stated without the model in the first place. Perhaps the model originally serves some heuristic function in thought, but formalists argue that it has no place in the body of science. For many people, however, the real heart of the understanding of science is in its models. We may not be able to grasp in its fullest complexity even something so simple in principle as a linear equation in n variables where n is a large number, but we may very well appreciate a spatial model of such a process when n is equal to three. We can generalize our understanding of this spatial model, to ones which have more than three dimensions. We can form a model of three dimensional space by drawing pictures or by simply having a visual image.

Because, in social sciences, understanding is as significant as the development of the logical consequences of some theory, metaphorical aspects of theories are important. It is doubtful whether anyone could derive certain, unambiguous implications from Freud's theoretical writings by the application of a rigorous logic. The metaphors—implicit in the very names Freud used, names such as *id* or *Oedipal complex*—are of fundamental importance to intellectual life in the twentieth century. Almost no aspect of the social sciences and humanities has been untouched by psychoanalytic theory. Furthermore, if Freud had avoided the metaphor in his theory and restricted himself to a rigorous logical development, his ideas would not have had the significance for modern man that they do. They are psychological theories cast in meta-

---

[4] Since the advent of computers, the model has come to be a bit more useful in formal science. In a computer simulation model, some complicated process, the exact formal derivation of which cannot be worked out in detail by a human being, is worked out by a computer. But the computer simulation process differs only from the more metaphorical models in the explicitness of the detail. It does not differ in the extent to which it falls short of complete justification in formal science.

phors of interpersonal relations, and that is one of the most important things about them.

In all science, models and diagrams (which are really kinds of models) have a role, simply because it is much easier to explain an idea to someone else if one can use a model. To a certain extent, therefore, all scientific theory conforms to the limitations of human understanding, but it is much more important for some psychological theories to do so than for physical theories. This is because there is something unique about psychological theories. The peculiar aspect of psychological theories emerges from a combination of the traditional view of psychology as the investigation of human consciousness and the more modern view that it is the study of behavior. The subject matter of psychology becomes a dual one. Psychological theory and data combine to make factual statements about human action, but psychology is also supposed to describe and explain what each of us recognizes inwardly in his own consciousness.

Because there is a dual subject matter, at least some psychological theorists recognize a dual obligation. Psychological theories by their view must not only meet the external demands of scientific validity, they must also be intuitively appealing. Most theories of personality, including that whole family of theories deriving from psychoanalysis, have such a dual allegiance. They respond both to the traditional values of science and to the values of internal validity provided by personal, human experience. The very fact that unconscious processes are central in such theories points up this state of affairs.

Many psychologists and philosophers of science are not in sympathy with the dual criterion. They regard the question of the intuitive validity of psychological theory as spurious. Thus, while psychoanalytic theory is metaphorical by nature, behavioristic theory is not. This inconsistency makes for a certain incommensurability among psychological theories, a fact that leads some observers to doubt that psychology can ever be a coherent discipline.

It certainly makes for different styles of doing psychology, but it is not chaos. There is less contradiction among rival psychological theories than appears on the surface, simply because rival theories are often addressed to different problems and obey different rules. Psychology, as an intellectual enterprise, remains vigorous as long as we recognize that there are different goals for different theories and as long as we do not exercise an intellectual fascism by ruling one or another criterion out of court.

3
INDUCTION

Induction is the defining characteristic for all empirical sciences and at the same time provides the greatest philosophical stumbling block for them. The basic goal of induction, reasoning from particular observations to general conclusions, is to make plausible the acceptance of a particular observation as universal. Since all empirical or scientific observations are particular, the problem is the most fundamental in the whole of science.

There are many ways in which particular psychological observations come to be accepted as more or less universal. We may assume, as many psychologists do, that the results of a particular psychological test characterize human beings in all situations in which the trait under consideration might conceivably be exhibited. The idea that a particular test can reveal a universal trait is basic to psychological testing. Another, totally different aspect of reasoning from the particular to the general concerns the reliability of observations. To reason from the particular, that is, "A saw a flying saucer" to the general, that is, "flying saucers exist" requires confirming observations from others. Here the question is not one of representativeness so much as it is a matter of stability. This latter problem is a universal one in science, and it has received the attention of statisticians. There is an armory of techniques suitable for assessing the reliability of the results of psychological testing and experimentation. Both of these aspects of induction—representativeness and reliability—are important questions to psychologists and will be examined in this chapter. Another aspect of inductive reasoning is far more basic, and it seldom receives the attention it deserves. It centers around the

44

common-sense view of causation held implicitly or explicitly by most investigators of psychological phenomena.

On cause and effect

The nature of causation has been a concern of philosophers since the seventeenth century. Classical and medieval philosophers believed that the concepts "cause" and "effect" stood for objective categories. But beginning in the seventeenth century and culminating in the eighteenth with the arguments advanced by David Hume, the whole question of whether cause and effect existed in the world or merely in the mind of human observers became central in philosophic discussion. Hume argued that cause and effect were merely the result of temporal covariation—the fact that one thing always *seemed*, in ordinary human experience, to follow another. Cause and effect were not in nature but in the experience of the observer. Immanuel Kant, the great eighteenth-century German philosopher who shaped so much of modern thought, solved the problem of causation in a way that most working scientists, including psychological scientists, would regard as highly unsatisfactory. He asserted that the relation of cause and effect was a property of the human mind. It was something that the mind imposed on the world and was not extrinsic to the observing mind.

Philosophers being philosophers, Kant's arguments did not settle the issue. Various philosophers since his time have tried to provide evidence for the objective existence of cause and effect. In the twentieth century, philosophers of science have produced detailed and sophisticated theories of cause and effect based on certain assumptions about the nature of the physical world and the human mind. Hans Reichenbach, a significant figure in the founding of logical positivism, made a careful analysis of the nature of cause and effect from the standpoint of the nature of time.[1] Because psychologists, as working scientists, are not concerned with the

---

[1] See H. Reichenbach, *The Direction of Time* (Berkeley, Calif.: University of California Press, 1956). Reichenbach argues that time is defined by thermodynamics, and hence, so are cause and effect.

ultimate nature of physical concepts (including what might be called objective time), many of the subtle and significant arguments advanced by Reichenbach about the nature of cause and effect are not terribly relevant to the problems the psychological investigator faces in his work. But some other philosophic conceptions are relevant. These are conceptions that have to do with the nature of the inference necessary to establish cause and effect relations from some empirical observation.

One view of cause and effect is the assertion that it is a relation exhibited between two events when certain criteria have been met by those events. It is sometimes said that in order to demonstrate a causal relation, the cause must be both *necessary* and *sufficient* to the effect. It is necessary because in order for B to occur, A must always occur; in the absence of A, B never happens. It is sufficient because B occurs every time A occurs; A never happens without B following. The application of the criteria of necessity and sufficiency to causative relations in actual observation is difficult and complicated. Philosophers may argue that these criteria can never be met in empirical research. But the psychologist's conception of causative relations is seldom as rigorous as that of the philosopher. The psychological investigator generally accepts the existence of a causative relation when two conditions covary regularly and repeatedly. In short, many investigators accept a causal relation as existing for precisely the reasons that Hume stated—temporal covariation. To show causation to the satisfaction of the empirical investigator, one must produce the same pair of events under a variety of circumstances and show that the relation between the pair is invariant (the same). This is possible only if A can be repeated, and if each time that A is repeated, B also occurs (which meets the criterion of necessity but not sufficiency). Literally, of course, no event can be repeated, but it is possible to produce a series of events having certain characteristics in common. The whole of empirical science depends on the assumption that at least the essential properties of one event can be duplicated in another. Saying that two events may occur repeatedly in covariation is thus only an approximation of the truth; what we mean is that the important features of a series of events are the same (invariant) for a number of repetitions.

Like the philosopher of science, the working scientist insists that one of the events, the cause, precedes the other, the effect. However, questions in the foundations of physics seldom worry the psychologist (unless he is concerned with such problems as extrasensory perception), and the notion of time as defined very crudely by classical physical operations is satisfactory to the psychologist. Implicit, then, in the psychologist's conception of the cause and effect relations is the view of one event as a reaction to another.

In practice, the psychologist's application of these criteria is even cruder and less rigorous than the conception outlined above would suggest. A simple example often used in the laboratory exercises for introductory psychology is a study of reaction time. The problem is to demonstrate that the time it takes to react to an auditory stimulus is influenced by the amount of time that elapses between the presentation of a warning signal and the presentation of the stimulus to which the subject is supposed to react. The term "influence" is meant to assert that something causes a change in something else. Variations in reaction time of a certain magnitude are said to be caused by, or influenced by, variations in the warning time, or preparation time. Most psychologists will accept some statistical evidence of a covariation between preparation time and reaction time as evidence for a causative relation. They will accept data demonstrating that on the *average*, shorter reaction times go with longer preparation times. For any particular event, however, no psychologist would be surprised to see the relation reversed. Such variations from what one would naively suppose to be a strict covariation are attributed to statistical or stochastic (random) conditions disturbing the basic relationship of influence or to the possibility that any given event has multiple causes. It is clear, therefore, that the psychologist is quite willing to accept a very loose linkage between an event that in whole or part causes one event and the reaction that follows.

One might suppose, given such a loose linkage, that psychologists would be pleased to dispose of the concept of causation altogether. In fact, they talk very little about causation as such. The phrase "cause and effect" is hardly mentioned in the writing of psychologists. But indirect evidence points to the central role given the concept of causation by psychologists. For instance, psychologists believe that those observations in which events are controlled are better than others. The reaction time example provides a case in point; something like it is often used in elementary textbooks to explain the superiority of the experimental method over other methods of observation. Preparation time is said to influence (cause changes in) reaction time because the investigator can show that when all other conditions are held constant (controlled) and the amount of warning time varied, reaction time changes. Of course, no experimenter can literally hold all conditions constant. There is an absolute difference between each and every observation. What the psychologist means by holding all things constant is that he has controlled all those aspects of the testing situation that his experience has taught him could conceivably influence reaction time.

Since psychology is not highly developed enough to tell us what conditions should be controlled, the psychologist relies largely on his intuition for this decision. Most psychologists would assume that if the reaction time apparatus were picked up and moved to a neighboring room, the relation between preparation time and reaction time would not be disturbed. On the other hand, if the ambient temperature of the room were raised from a normal 70 degrees to 130 degrees Fahrenheit, the relation between preparation and reaction time might well be disturbed. A great deal of intuition enters into the notion of a control, intuition that is not specifiable in psychological theory but that is the common inheritance of all those who do psychological research. Novices— new graduate students—are often much more concerned about controlling all the conditions in the psychological laboratory than are experienced experimenters. So, in point of fact, we may say that psychologists are willing to grant a high status to covariation when even just *some* of the conditions of observations are controlled. The decision of what to control is generally the result of vague and unspecified common sense and experience.

All of this may seem quite far from the logical criteria for establishing causation, but at bottom the psychological experiment represents the attempts of the psychologist as investigator to approximate these criteria. The superiority in making causal inferences that psychologists grant to the experimental testing situation makes that method preeminent among psychological methods, even when the rigor associated with the notion of control is lost in intuitive decision. Controlled observation is regarded as the highest state of empirical investigation. In controlled observation, not only are the conditions of testing made reliable, but a small number of conditions are singled out as causative variables and deliberately changed.

The concept of cause in psychological theory

Although most psychologists make do with a naive and simple view of causation, psychological research would be improved by a more considered conception. There is no reason for the psychologist to adopt the skepticism of Hume, but he should free himself from the belief that he is making use of a particularly powerful inferential tool in experimentation when in fact he is not. A better abstract structure than that of cause and effect for understanding the consequences of psychological investigation is the notion of covariation among conditions that are embedded in a matrix of other covariations, all of which make up a large network of relations, partly empirical and partly theoretical. Causation as an inference then arises not from direct observation but from the plausibility of the whole empirical-theoretical structure. A more sophisticated approach would not place the burden of causative inference—as is traditionally the case—on the covariation of an independent and dependent variable but on the analysis of the interrelationships within a set of propositions, some of which are empirical and some of which are theoretical. The problem of what causes what becomes part of the whole theoretical problem that motivates the investigation in the first place.

The development of such an approach to causation can be illustrated by an example. The example is a real one taken from the observations of an experimental psychologist.[2] At first the problem might seem to be as trivial as the one of reaction time, but it has more fundamental implications that derive in large part from more sophisticated views about how to go about the business of psychological investigation.

The situation under investigation is somewhat as follows: A human subject is placed in an isolation booth in a psychology laboratory. He looks at a series of pairs of sentences, and from each pair he is supposed to choose one to read. After he reads the sentence of his choice, a stream of cool air may be blown across his forehead. This is an important circumstance, since the chamber is kept at a temperature of 110 degrees Fahrenheit and 35 percent humidity. It happens that the draft of cool air is correlated with some peculiar property of the sentence. For example, it may occur whenever the subject chooses a sentence having plural rather than singular nouns as subjects. The psychological problem is twofold. It is first of all to determine how often the subject makes the "correct" choice. More important, however, it is to determine what the subject makes of this situation. This will be determined by (1) what the subject thinks about the experiment, (2) the conditions of the experiment, (3) how these conditions are varied, and (4) how the subject reacts to his own reactions. One way in which we can make reasonable inferences about the psychological causes of a subject's decision in this experiment is to vary the conditions. What, for example, does the subject do when he is allowed to invent sentences on his own? Does he invent sentences with plural nouns as subjects in order to receive this "reinforcing" stimulus? Even more important, we ought to find out what the subject *believes* about the situation. Does he, for example, choose sentences according to what he believes to be the motives behind the blast of cool air? In order to find that out, we may have to question the subject. One way to question him is to ask him to write down his reactions to the situation. Another, perhaps more reliable, method is to ask him to fill out a questionnaire. In short,

[2] D. E. Dulany, "Awareness, Rules and Propositional Control: A Confrontation with S-R Behavior Therapy," in T. R. Dixon and D. L. Horton, *Verbal Behavior and General Behavior Therapy* (Englewood Cliffs, N.J.: Prentice-Hall, 1968).

we use a variety of techniques, all of which are interrelated and which are devised to determine with some degree of plausibility the essentials of the subject's reactions as well as his attitudes and beliefs.

The experimenter may believe that the changes in the responses of the subject in this situation are caused by what the subject thinks about, the conditions of reinforcement, the conditions of motivation (how unpleasant the environment is), and a number of other circumstances. But the experimenter does not attempt to produce experimental control over the thinking processes of the subject. Rather, he examines the interrelations among the patterns of responses and what he can determine about the beliefs of the subject from questionnaire data. He studies the structure of a pattern of interrelated variables. The cause and effect relation is in the experimenter's theory, not in the data obtained in an experiment. The plausibility of the theory is not so much at the mercy of the degree to which the experimental conditions match the requirements of necessity and sufficiency as they are at the mercy of the coherence of the structural relations among the various conditions of the experiment. In short, do all the inter-relations that the experimenter is capable of studying add up to a view of what causes what?

The moral of this example is that the burden of causative inference should not be placed on induction, least of all on the assumption that one kind of situation is inherently better for making inductive inferences than any other. There are techniques of observation that are appropriate to a given problem, and the appropriateness of the techniques has nothing to do with whether or not that science is experimental. Astronomy is no less highly determined and well-developed a science than physics. In fact, physics and astronomy were indistinguishable as the major source of data for the great principles of mechanics that became the foundation of Newtonian theory. Some of the most important observations were derived from astronomical observation rather than from the classical model of experimentation in physics. Whether a psychologist can make a good case for his particular notion of what causes what depends not so much on whether he uses the experimental method as it does on the plausibility of a whole set of theoretical and empirical relations of which a single experiment may be only a small part.

The distinction between independent and dependent variables —in which the independent variables are outside of the organism and the dependent variables are responses of the organism—is not of critical importance. Similarly, the distinction between stimulus variables and response variables is of little methodological significance. At one time some psychologists made much of the difference between what they called response-response laws and stimulus-response laws. The so-called response-response laws were supposed to be based on correlations between responses, while the stimulus-response laws were based on controlled stimuli that produced responses. This distinction was never rigorously adhered to even by those who advocated it. In some studies of verbal learning, for example, the ability of subjects to learn meaningful material and meaningless material might be compared. The difference between the two kinds of materials constitutes an independent variable, and since these materials are presented to the subjects, they are, by the behavioral methodologist's notion, stimuli. Thus, such an experiment should lead to some stimulus-response law. But the important difference between the stimuli (the meaningfulness of the verbal materials) is determined by how people react to them in different situations. That is how the experimental psychologist tells whether or not the material is meaningful. Viewed this way, such an experiment is really an effort to discover some response-response law in which the responses from one group of subjects predict responses from other subjects. In fact, the whole analysis that leads to the contrast between stimulus-response laws and response-response laws is useless and impossible to maintain in such situations. Ultimately, of course, it is rooted in a naive notion of causation.

Causative inference belongs to a theory about something, not to the data obtained or to results of that theory. A theory makes the statements about what is necessary and sufficient for the production of certain events. It will say what is supposed to influence what. Observation then provides a structural description of the world that, in some way, should correspond to the description arrived at by the theory. Theories have different kinds of empirical consequences. They lead to different kinds of descriptions of the world. Some theories are much more useful than others. Among the most useful theories are those that make strong statements about cause and effect relations and at the same time are well integrated into a total structure that includes broadly based and reliable empirical information.

Correlational data and causation

From time to time it has been claimed that correlational studies do not lead to strong causative inferences. Often they do not, but not for the reasons ordinarily given. They do not lead to strong causal inferences because they are not usually articulated as part of theories that have well-organized structural properties. This fact may be illustrated by a methodological trick that psychologists have borrowed from economists—time-lagged or cross-lagged correlations. Many demographic characteristics may be studied by comparing a pattern of correlations over time. For example, various indices of business activity are correlated with marriage rate. The higher the index of business activity in any given period, the higher, on the average, the marriage rate. There is nothing in such a relationship, of course, that makes it more likely that one is the fundamental cause than the other. A theory—that is, a set of plausible hypotheses—could easily be defended on either side. One could argue that people wait to get married until business conditions are good. One could also argue that when people marry younger and thus produce higher marriage rates, there is a greater demand on the economy, which results in an increase in the various indices of business activity. On the face of it, there is little to make one of these notions more plausible than the other. But one can expand either of these theories by introducing the concept of time lag. This leads to a result that may differentiate between them.

Suppose one argues that influences—what causes what—take an appreciable period of time to develop. The social system is a viscous one, and it takes a long time for changes to have influence.

Therefore, if marriage rates are to have an effect on business prosperity, some appreciable time must elapse between an increase in marriage rates and an increase in business activity. On the other hand, if business activity is to influence marriage rates, a similar time lag must occur in the reverse direction. This now enables a slightly stronger test of the causative hypothesis, because one can now correlate marriage rates lagged, say, six months or a year behind indices of business activities, and one can also examine the correlation when the figures for business conditions are taken six months or so after those for marriage rates. The higher correlation will occur, the argument goes, when the true cause, or the more important or significant cause, leads. If marriage rates have the primary influence, the correlation should be higher when marriage rates lead indices of business activity than when marriage rates lag.

The use of such auxiliary hypotheses with correlational information is quite highly developed, much more so than this example may suggest.[3] A very sophisticated use of correlational data in establishing the truth or falsity of theoretical propositions about causation is possible. In simple fact, however, the method is just an extension of the notion that makes causative inferences plausible from experimental data, the idea that temporal priority is an important part of the theory of what causes what. Whenever an assumption of temporal priority and its empirical demonstration make an inference about causation more plausible, such an assumption is justified.

The problem in making any causative inference is one of finding appropriate and relevant observations. It is not possible, for example, to test theories of inheritance of abilities in man in a very significant way because it is not possible to make observations about the variations in experience of human beings with identical genetic character. We need identical genetic character not because of the need to "control" but because genetic theory cannot tell us in detail precisely how any two human beings differ in genetic structure. Without the availability of critical data, the observations simply cannot be made. The properties of necessity and sufficiency

3 See R. M. Rozelle and D. T. Campbell, "More Plausible Rival Hypotheses in Cross-lagged Panel Correlation Technique," *Psychological Bulletin*, 1969, 71, 74–80.

properly belong in theory, not in the technique of empirical investigation.

Statistics and inductive inference

The reliability of information obtained through observation is assessed though the application of statistical theory. In the late nineteenth century and in the twentieth century, statistics as an applied science developed on a foundation of probability theory. Among other things, statistics enabled experimental investigators to make stringent tests of the *reliability* of the results of their experiments. Statistical theory assumes that each observation or individual measurement is subject to influences that cause errors. These influences are large in number and independent, and each is small in the extent of its influence. (These errors of measurement have nothing to do with such subjective factors as our views of what the outcome should be, nor are they influenced by whatever previous observations we might have made.) Variations among observations result from these random influences affecting each observation. The precision of any result is decreased by the variability among the observations and increased by the number of observations. Statistical theory tells us that the reliability of observations is proportional to the square root of their number. The more observations there are, the more random influences there will be. And statistical theory holds that the more random errors there are, the more they are likely to cancel one another and produce a *normal distribution*. A normal distribution is simply the mathematical consequence of a large number of independent factors contributing to error each in a small way.

All statistical inference is based on distributions. The small, independent influences that lead to error are generally assumed to be the conditions that produce distributions of observations. A number of types of distributions are known to statisticians, each of which has some special property. The most familiar one is the normal distribution. Errors of observations are normally distributed. But early in the history of modern statistics it was discovered that very small samples (or a small number of observations resulted in distributions that were not normal, even though larger samples would lead to error with normal distributions. Means or averages of observations based on small samples are subject to errors that are not normally distributed.

The use of such unreliable samples is sometimes a necessity—psychological data are often difficult and expensive to obtain. Statisticians have suggested various ways of deciding how much to trust summaries based on small numbers of observations subject to fluctuations. They have called on a fundamental aspect of their theory in so doing. As with so many fundamental questions there is no uniform agreement among theorists, so different decision procedures are suggested by different statisticians. However, very influential in psychology and used almost to the exclusion of any other is the procedure generally known as *hypothesis testing*.

Hypothesis testing is peculiarly appropriate to psychology because it is especially designed for problems in which only a small number of observations can be made. Hypothesis-testing statistics are sometimes known as small-sample statistics. The statistician's small-sample theory requires the testing of fixed, exact hypotheses. One cannot confidently use small samples to establish a range of possible outcomes, but one can test exact hypotheses. Paradoxical as it may seem at first, it is easier to test the adequacy of a fixed hypothesis with the use of small samples than to show what the limits are on some very general result. The most widely used exact hypothesis is the *null hypothesis*. The null hypothesis states that the true value in some infinite population of observations is zero. In a particular case, the null hypothesis might assert that there is a zero mean difference (that is, no difference) between two conditions. In another case it might assert that the true correlation between two conditions—say, marriage rate and business activity figures, mentioned earlier—is zero.

Let us consider the case of comparison of two means or averages. This is a common kind of comparison in psychological research. Usually, the purpose of comparing two conditions is to establish that there *is* a difference between them, so to begin with the null hypothesis appears to be perverse and contrary. But one way to view an experimental test is to say that it is aimed at *rejecting* the null hypothesis. If there is a sufficiently large difference between some experimental condition and control, then the null hypothesis can be rejected. If one rejects the null hypothesis, one concludes that because it is unlikely that there is *no* difference, there is in fact *some* difference. This rather Byzantine mode of argument is commonly accepted among psychologists and others who employ small samples in research. Nearly every psychological experiment results in some statement to the effect that the null hypothesis can be rejected at the .05 level of confidence (or the .01 level of confidence). These statements about levels of confidence refer to the probability that the rejection of the null hypothesis is *incorrect*. If we reject the null hypothesis at the 5 percent level of confidence, we are likely to be right 95 percent of the time and wrong 5 percent of the time. This means that we are willing to accept a 5 percent chance of being wrong in rejecting the null hypothesis. One can only reject an exact hypothesis, and the rejection is always at a specified level of confidence. In empirical investigation in any field the investigator never knows whether the obtained result is *exactly* correct. The level of confidence states his willingness to make errors of a particular kind with a fixed probability. Thus if he wants to accept a lower rate of error, he might hold out for the 1 percent level of confidence rather than the 5 percent.

Despite the almost universal acceptance among psychologists of hypothesis testing, particularly of testing the null hypothesis, this is seldom what psychological experiments are all about. Psychologists rarely want merely to establish that there is an absence of no difference between two conditions. Rather, investigators would prefer to say that the difference between two conditions is of a particular magnitude—in effect, the magnitude found in a particular comparison. Even though every researcher knows that a particular obtained result cannot be *exactly* correct, nearly all investigators believe their result to be close to what would be found if the investigation were performed again. Thus, if an investigator finds that the mean number of errors made by rats in solving a problem increased, on the average, ten times following a removal of a portion of the brain, he accepts the exact figure (ten times) as being approximately correct. By "approximately correct" he means that if he did the experiment again, he would find a result of a similar order of magnitude. Thus, the testing of an exact hypothesis, particularly the null hypothesis, is generally a fiction. It is not a useless fiction, though, for the method does provide a way for the empirical scientist to assess the reliability of his results. Much empirical information in psychology is less reliable than it ought to be. The reliability of data is inversely proportional to the square root of the number of observations. In order to reject the null hypothesis at some fixed level of confidence, a larger number of observations will be required for data that are highly variable than for data that are not highly variable. But the testing of exact hypotheses, particularly the testing of null hypotheses, has enabled psychologists to use smaller samples than they would use if they were completely without self-delusion about the reliability of their results. For most purposes, hypothesis testing should be replaced by the estimation of confidence intervals. This requires the use of statistical inference to estimate within what range one may expect the true value resulting from some observations—the obtained values of which will surely vary from occasion to occasion—to occur. In short, statistics should tell us within what range we are *approximately* correct. The estimation of confidence intervals also requires larger samples—given classical ways of doing experiments—than psychologists are willing or often able to use.

An even more fundamental problem, however, concerns the application of statistical inference itself. The application of statistical inference requires a model about data that assumes some random (stochastic) variability imposed on a fixed (nonstochastic) result. This conception has profoundly influenced the psychologist's view of nature and has entered the very substance of modern psychological theory. One widely accepted view asserts that there are fixed psychological laws or principles and that these result in empirical principles that can be precisely stated. But to determine whether or not these principles are true, one must resort to averaging a large number of observations. The averaging of a large number of observations is necessary because random errors of various sorts, including those of measurement and those from uncontrolled conditions, disturb the fixed results. Thus, the typical psychological theory concerns fixed, or nonstochastic, events that are perturbed by uncontrolled conditions of observation. This is by no means the only possible way to view psychological principles. There are psychological theories that incorporate statistical variability directly into the underlying principles themselves, but the typical conception of a psychological result or psychological theory is deterministic rather than stochastic or statistical. It is quite possible that deterministic theories are inappropriate to much of psychology. In any event the traditional use of statistical inference in psychology has encouraged psychologists to be content with average results obtained from highly variable data.

Sampling: making the particular stand for the general

Sampling entails the problem of how to make the particular stand for the general. A small group of particular college sophomores is often used as though it were representative of a large population—for example, college sophomores at large or even human beings at large. The notion of sampling permeates psychological thinking, and most psychologists now recognize that sampling applies to things other than simply the people or animals tested in an experiment. Some particular set of conditions in an experiment is generally taken to be representative of all possible conditions of a similar type. For example, psycholinguists are often interested in how people remember ordinary sentences. The thirty or forty actual sentences used in a particular psycholinguistic experiment on remembering sentences are supposed to represent all possible sentences in the English language. So, in a sense, an experiment of this sort entails sampling not only people, but the English language as well.

In one important respect, the concept of sampling has been neglected where it might well be applied. Sampling theory also should be applied to the situations necessary in order to test a theory. Consider the investigation of altruism once again. In the investigation of altruism, situations are devised to permit people to make altruistic choices. Usually a single situation provides the setting for the experimental testing. The particular test situation may be one in which a subject is given the opportunity to come to the aid of someone else. That situation may be advertised as one in which it is possible to "measure" altruistic behavior. Though the experimenter may not say so explicitly, often that situation is implicitly understood to be representative of all possible (or a vaguely unspecified number of) situations in which people can make altruistic choices. The experimenter may be very careful to test an adequate number of subjects and perhaps to control and vary aspects of the particular experimental situation. But he will allow that one particular situation to stand for all the unspecified circumstances in which an individual could be altruistic. There are a thousand variations on any particular example of this situation. Are other people present? If so, how many? Are they peers or strangers? How does the subject (victim) interpret the situation? What are the conditions that are likely to change his interpretation? Any attempt to sample all *relevant* conditions would be quixotic and foolish unless the experimenter could rely on a highly developed, plausible, and very general theory of altruism. Then, the ability of the sampling to represent the range of altruistic situations would depend, among other things, on the theory. All too often, however, the social psychologist as experimenter is content to let a particular situation stand for an indefinite range of possible testing situations in a vague and unspecified way.

There are alternatives other than sampling theory to the problem of sampling appropriate psychological situations. As we have just seen, the relation between the theory and the observation is of critical importance. If the theory and observation are explicitly related to one another through some rigorous logical process, then the sampling of conditions may become completely unnecessary. It is unnecessary because the theory is rigorously related to a particular experimental or observational test as well as to other, and perhaps all, appropriate situations. The theory, then, rather than sampling, tells us whether or not to expect in some particular new situation the same result found in an old one. Furthermore, the theory should tell us what kinds of situations can be encompassed in a generalization. If psychological investigation were truly rigorous, the answer to that question would too often be "none."

But a theory having such power is almost never found in psychology, and so, by default, psychologists imply that they are sampling some condition such as altruism by means of a particular observation. That this is implicit rather than explicit is revealed by the fact that psychologists, who should know better, will allow one or at the most two or three observations to stand for all possible conditions. Another difficulty with this implicit conception is that the sampling limits are vague. This in itself is by no means unusual. In fact, in a psychological experiment or a psychological observation, sampling ranges are nearly always vague and indefinite. College sophomores are the subjects for countless experiments, but few psychologists intend their results to be limited to college sophomores. Rather, they suppose that they are studying some process in human beings at large. It provides another instance of the fact that much of experimental psychology is based on unarticulated intuition and assumption. Sometimes, perhaps, it is not terribly important whether the assumption is correct or not, but at other times, when some process such as altruism is at stake, it surely is.

The relation between theory and data

Most people regard the most important aspect of science to be the collection of data. In a sense this attitude is correct. It is the essential contribution of the scientific point of view as opposed to pure rationalism to insist on information of an empirical sort. It is this characteristic that sets empirical sciences off from logic and mathematics, on the one hand, and purely evaluative disciplines, such as literary criticism or ethics, on the other. Despite the essential reliance of psychology, as with any science, on observation, empirical information plays a more modest role than we might suppose. The function of empirical observation is not to find out what causes what, or the truth about some aspects of nature, or how things work in some ultimate sense, but simply to provide justification for some particular way of looking at the world. Observation justifies a theory, a method, or an attitude or point of view. It is the function of empirical information to tell us how *adequate* our notions are about what causes what, about the true nature of things, or about how things work. It does so simply by enabling us to tell whether one conception is better than another, viewed from where we stand right now.

Because scientific theories are evaluated by comparing them with other available theories, and not by their absolute merits, it often happens that a particular way of looking at things (if the theory is loose and informal), or a genuine theory (if the theory is formal and logically consistent) persists long beyond the point at which everyone is convinced that it is wrong or insufficient. It persists because of the absence of effective competition. At least some psychologists regard such a state of affairs to be the present condition of psychoanalytic theory. Perhaps it has outlived its usefulness, but there is no theory of personality and personality development with anywhere near the power to replace it, so it still occupies a virtually unchallenged role in the psychology of personality. Whatever competition the original Freudian conceptions have comes from Jung, Horney, and Erikson, all of whom worked within the framework set by Freud.

The notion that theories may be demolished by empirical evidence is, by and large, historically incorrect. Only rigorously derived theories that are grossly out of line with evidence suffer such a fate. It is in general the wrong way to use empirical knowledge to expect it to "test" a theory. Empirical information cannot itself provide the framework of a science, nor can it be used to demolish an existing framework. The framework of a science is provided by the integrated set of propositions that make up a theory. One theory cannot be displaced by facts; it can be displaced only by another theory, a theory that gives rise to more comprehensive facts, more useful facts, or, simply, newer facts. It sometimes happens that a new theory, viewed in a dispassionate and independent way, may be little better than an old theory. It may, however, generate a new set of facts or emphasize a new set of methods and thus be more fashionable.[4] The reasons for the displacement of one view or theory in psychology by another are

---

[4] There are fashions and fads in science. New problems, new techniques, and new theories have a fascination beyond whatever merit they may have by some strict scientific accounting procedure.

often hard to determine. Historically, the displacement of the traditional introspective view in experimental psychology by behaviorism was more on promise than anything else. Behaviorism drew its strength from the new kinds of observations it suggested, rather than from what it had actually accomplished. It attracted attention and became fashionable.

Sometimes empirical information is misused in the absence of theory. We have just seen that simple observations about some particular condition in the laboratory (or in a naturalistic setting) can be blown up to reach conclusions of a most general nature. Not everyone remembers that the original observations were limited to a very particular situation. Investigators take it on faith that the conditions described in the laboratory are to be generalized more or less at large. The intuitive and free-ranging application of the results of such studies provides the substance of what amounts to a kind of underground theory in psychology. The real basis for many of the generalizations that appear in textbooks and other places is intuition and speculation of the flimsiest sort built on the base of a few rather limited and often highly specialized observations.

Genuine empirical observations of great generality are rare and limited mainly to purely descriptive matters. Much of descriptive geology and comparative anatomy of past generations is closer to being genuine empirical science than almost anything else. But neither of these subjects is really motivated by its purely descriptive functions. The matters of deepest scientific interest in both anatomy and geology are theoretical in nature, derived from theories about the history of our planet. They have become part of a general theoretical structure concerned with the evolution of the universe in the case of geology and with organic evolution in the case of comparative anatomy.

In psychology there are occasional instances of empirical results that seem to be used almost entirely without presupposition and that do not favor one theory or another. For example, a common use of tests of intellectual ability is to predict, say, achievement in college, or college dropout rate. Very little psychological theory enters into such predictions. What theory there is comes from a theory of statistics rather than of psychology. A test is devised that incorporates some of the principles of applied statistics as these have been developed in test-construction theory. This test is given to a sample of individuals, carefully designed to be representative of some particular population. We correlate the results of the test—again using methods developed in applied statistics—with indices of academic achievement in college. If there is a correlation, the test may be used to predict achievement (with a margin of error). The whole theory of prediction is statistical, not psychological.

Those who would want to generalize the results of such a study over time—say, to apply information obtained in 1939 to 1969—are again making use of some kind of intuitively derived theory. Among other things, the theory would imply that the essential nature of the relationship between intellectual ability and achievement in college has not changed despite the large change in college population. But there is no way of knowing whether such an assumption is correct without redoing the whole study and bringing it up to date.

If we follow the principles of induction literally, we are limited to generalizations based on the single assumption that an observation or a series of observations made at a particular time is representative of another set of observations that might be made at another time. By representative we mean that the essential features under study will have remained unchanged. We may not even specify what those features are, but may simply make the assumption that the condition remains unchanged. Thus, the basis of an attempt at empirical generalization lies, not in any particular scientific theory, but in the theory of induction as it has been developed in its most useful and complete form in the theory of statistics. The limits of empirical generalization correspond to the kinds of limitations placed on observation by statistical theory. But most problems demand more than purely statistical assumptions. The use in 1969 of a test validated in 1939 makes the implicit assumption that the relevant psychological and sociological conditions have remained unchanged over that period.

Practical scientific problems are subject to the same limitations as those of purely theoretical interest. Even the most mundane problem demands that we entertain some theory—however "implied"—if we are to solve it. There is a tendency in psychology today, however, to believe that both practical problems and those of theoretical interest can be resolved by appeals to evidence. One well-known contemporary example is provided by the argument about the origins of group differences (particularly racial) in intelligence. Are race or sex differences in abilities a reflection of the different experiences one group has had compared with another, or are they caused by inherited factors? There is a persistent feeling among psychologists and others that this question and similar ones ought to be answerable empirically. Most people seem to think that the answer to the question should come not from theory, but from the examination of data. From time to time the available data, generally based on intelligence test scores, are examined in an attempt to settle the question. But the data are inadequate for such a task. They always will be inadequate because such questions are answerable only on the basis of certain assumptions, which constitute a theory of sorts.

The recent controversy over a publication by Jensen [5] on differences between white and black Americans is a case in point. The argument is supposed to center around the adequacy of empirical data that Jensen summarizes. In fact, the real source of argument is with the theory of intelligence and human genetics behind Jensen's argument. However central the role of data in science, the interpretation of scientific facts depends on theory and assumption. What is important about any scientific activity are the ideas or conceptions that are part of that activity. The role of the empirical data is to provide grounds for the advocacy of one or another set of ideas in an ongoing debate. The points of view from which the debate is carried out—that is, the positions that are defended—are the central matters at issue. These are theories, attitudes, and beliefs. Arguments about data are impossible. They nearly always turn out to be arguments about the adequacy of some theory for the collection of data. One scientist may say to another, "I don't believe your data." What he means by this is not that he does not believe the particular observations that another scientist has made, but that he believes the arguments

[5] A. L. Jensen, "How Much Can We Boost IQ and Scholastic Achievement?" *Harvard Educational Review*, 1969, 39, 1–123.

that make those data relevant to the question under consideration to be false. Thus, in the debate on the relation between genetic and environmental influences on intelligence, the data themselves are only superficially the cause of argument. One investigator may accuse another of gathering data with faulty sampling techniques. What he means is that the appropriate theory of sampling—the portion of statistical theory that applies to the gathering of empirical data and making inferences from a particular sample to the general case—does not fit the particular set of data in question. In short, the sample is inadequate not from any general considerations, but from those that specifically derive from sampling theory. So arguments about data hinge on such questions as the relevance and adequacy of the data for the theory they are supposed to represent and the way the data match particular theoretical issues. Data cannot be evaluated in any absolute way, but can only be evaluated with respect to the issues for which they are said to argue.

There is a shuttling back and forth between data and theory in psychology. It is sometimes said that the purpose of scientific theory is to generate data. We have just argued that the purpose of data is to provide defense for one or another scientific argument. This apparent mutual dependence of data and theory is a real one. But what happens to theories that make no contact with data or facts? Theories with no empirical consequences have a peculiar status in psychology. They cannot properly be said to be myths even in the most general sense, for myths often have empirical consequences. Every now and then one will find in the psychological journals a reasonably well organized theoretical statement—that is, one in which the assertions and propositions are free from internal contradiction—that seems to have few or no empirical consequences. Such a theory is in a sense scientific (as opposed to mythical), but it is a scientific theory stillborn. It has no consequences. The theory may be an idle application of mathematical argument to conceptions that are real enough, but for which the arguments may be irrelevant. Thus, there is a question of relevancy in science. Relevancy in science refers to the extent to which the empirical propositions are developed and the availability of methods for producing data that test those propositions. Some scientific theories are relevant in this sense and others are not. Sometimes humanistic theories are irrelevant in the same way scientific theories are. They have no consequences other than to make us happy or sad, true believers or skeptics.

The relation between
data and facts

In evaluating the role of empirical evidence in psychological research one must examine the relation between data and facts. Data are not facts in the ordinary sense. They are part of the information needed to establish psychological facts. Psychological facts are more than data, for they must include some theory—that is, information that arises independently of the collection of data. Put another way, psychological facts depend on the interpretation of data. This point is at times obscured because, in some research, data and facts are not clearly separated. Observations—or, more properly, the records resulting from observations—sometimes incorporate both theory and data. This is most obvious when a human observer interprets some observation, but it also happens when a mechanical device records the data. The very nature of the device itself reflects some preconception about the nature of the information it is to receive. Facts occur when data are interpreted to make them relevant to a theory or to some system of beliefs or attitudes. Although in theory data and facts may be separated, in practice unaided human observation inextricably binds them.

A clear example of an observation in which data and theory are not separated occurs in field observation of animal behavior, an activity that has come to be called *ethology*. The word "ethology" refers to the science of behavior. But it is now used to describe observations of animal behavior under more or less natural conditions. Thus, an investigator who studies chimpanzees in their natural surroundings, or tigers in the wild, or even the behavior of some domestic animal, such as the cat, in its natural habitat, is an ethologist. Although some ethological observation is done in the laboratory and some is done by recording instruments of various sorts, in general, ethologists simply observe in a natural setting.

Grooming, a kind of social behavior peculiar to primates, may be an object of such observation. It is behavior in which one animal vigorously inspects the coat of another monkey for bits and particles of dead skin, insects, and so on. The word "grooming" applied to this action has already prejudiced the observation. Thus, the statement that rhesus monkeys "groom" one another is a statement of fact, but it is also a statement that goes beyond the simple observation that there is a certain kind of behavior between two members of the same species. It gives a name to the action in a way that implies that the interaction between the two is social in nature and of a particular variety. Thus, the ethologist's description already includes a considerable amount of interpretation.

A psychotherapist observing the actions and speech of a patient also collects observations in a more or less natural setting. Like the ethologist, the clinical psychologist or the psychiatrist interprets as he observes. Even if a neutral observer—an independent investigator—observes a psychotherapist and his patient interacting with one another, there is still an interpretation of what happens. The same behavior could be recorded in a more neutral way—for example, by motion pictures or video tape. The film or tape provides a reservoir from which data may be extracted. A technician—or even a properly designed machine—can count the instances of some particular movement by the patient or the therapist. The record would then consist of the number of movements made by the two participants per unit of time. Such a record would comprise data. And such data would be far more neutral than the observation, for example, that the patient scratched himself whenever the therapist asked a question. But even data so mechanically recorded are not entirely neutral. The decision to tabulate certain data and not others already shows a prejudice that derives from theory or, more usually, from intuition. Thus the decision to tabulate movements (as opposed, say, to vocalizations) already implies some preconception about what is important or relevant in the situation.

One of the best-known examples of laboratory equipment

meant to collect data in a neutral way is the Skinner box. This is a small box into which a rat is placed and allowed free movement. A lever projects into the box, and the box is so arranged that there is a contingency between movement of the lever and some other event, such as the presentation of a pellet of food. If the rat is hungry, it very quickly learns that such a contingency exists. As the rat learns this fact, it presses the lever more and more until it achieves a high and steady rate. A record of the movement of the lever provides objective data to support the inference that the rat has learned. Learning in this case is indicated by a change of rate. A standard version of this result is the cumulative learning curve that appears in the section on conditioning and learning in almost all elementary textbooks in psychology.

This example is singled out because, on occasion, some psychologists have claimed that such behavioral data are completely objective. The statement is sometimes made that the presentation of such records from an experiment is free from interpretation and thus free of theory. It is not, of course. The particular form in which the data are presented—in fact, the selection of some particular data such as lever presses—implies a particular purpose. The extent to which it is possible to contrast a difference between observation and data lies in the extent to which interpretation can be separated from raw materials. Ideally, a completely neutral collection of data would imply no selection whatever. If there were no selection, it would be possible to recover completely the information available in the initial investigation. Any selection of data limits the availability of data and thus does include some interpretation. We do not record, for example, whether the rat presses the lever with his right paw, with his left paw, or with his teeth. The record does already make some interpretation of what is going on: in this case, it is the lever-food contingency that is important, and not the particular response. But even a record of an event such as a lever press permits a certain amount of freedom, and thus must be regarded as intermediate between data and observation. In order to be interpreted further, some additional information is required. We have to know that the lever press is about something, that it is, in fact, evidence that the animal *knows* the lever-food contingency. In many observations, as in the ethological field studies mentioned above, it simply may not be possible to separate a record from observation.

When data are collected, they are collected for a particular purpose, and that purpose, of course, derives from the investigator's ideas about what he is looking for. In short, the data depend on either theory or hunch. Thus, one theory has led a group of investigators to collect information about the force with which the lever is depressed in a Skinner box, while another group of investigators, under the guidance of another theory, regards the physical aspects of the response as supremely unimportant. The difference is in the theoretical preconception that the investigator carries into the situation with him. The selection of data is always determined by some preconception. Sometimes psychologists and other social scientists become concerned about the possible influence of such preconceptions and try to record "everything." If, however, an investigator attempts to record "everything" (say, by video tape), he may find himself so overburdened with records that it is impossible to make use of the material he has assembled. He cannot avoid some sort of predetermination of what is to be observed in a particular situation. Even so, records are not facts, only the raw materials for facts. Thus, the lever presses of the rat in the box do not constitute a psychological fact. It is a fact, however, that rats can learn contingencies of the sort investigated in the Skinner box.

It is often said that the function of science is to gather facts. This statement is more sensible than it first appears once we realize that facts are not simply completely neutral observations of nature, but are themselves highly prejudiced by the preconceptions of investigators and are derived from highly selective treatment of data. Piling up facts endlessly, however, quickly becomes more trouble than it is worth. Some areas in psychology are so overburdened with facts in this sense that any scientific use of them becomes almost impossible. The trouble is that such facts have not been assimilated into a broader intellectual context. Unassimilated facts have long reigned in the field of verbal learning. Here, various facts about how people learn combinations of nonsense syllables by rote have been gathered ad infinitum without arriving at any broad consensus about how such facts fit into our general concerns about the nature of the human mind.

We have examined the view that says behavior constitutes the subject matter of psychology. It is true that data concerning behavior are the raw materials out of which psychological fact is made. But the extent to which we characterize the entire enterprise as the study of behavior is the extent to which we commit ourselves to a total neutralization of psychology. It depends on how much we delude ourselves into believing that psychologists are engaged in the process of the unprejudiced gathering of data. The gathering of data is a very limited enterprise, and psychology as the study of behavior must be also viewed as a very limited enterprise.

The limits of induction

This portrait of the role of induction and empirical evidence in psychology is very different from that usually given in textbook accounts of psychological method. The view that observation, or science in general, consists simply of reasoning from the particular to the general is simplistic rather than wrong. The purpose of empirical evidence is to give rise to fact. But fact consists of a conjunction of data and theory. Science is, above all, distinguished by the presence of facts in this sense. Theory in the absence of data is not science in the accepted sense, and that is why statements about the factual distinguish scientific enterprises from other intellectual activities that give rise to theory but have no empirical concern. Very highly reasoned, abstract, indeed mathematical, theorizing may occur in a variety of disciplines that are not scientific in nature.

But it should be equally clear that data alone do not make a science. Data only give a science something to be about. The structure of psychological theory is like the intellectual structure of theology or mathematics, but it differs from these in that it is designed to form a union with information about the world. The conjunction of ideas and data produces the facts that are the ends of science. Once we realize this, the peculiar status of psychological observations becomes clear. Whether or not introspection, or the report of our subjective state of mind, is scientific is no longer a question of data; it is a question of the conjunction of theory and data. To ask if it is possible to use introspective evidence as data is not a proper question because such a question already shows that we have a particular preconception as to what the facts are going to be. Even if we regard introspection as having some kind of unique epistemological status, the role of introspective fact in psychology is entirely dependent on the role it plays in a particular psychological theory.

If we say that fact is a mixture of data and theory, then we must differentiate between the reliability and the value of the facts. The intellectual value of any particular fact comes from the plausibility of the theory behind the fact, not necessarily from the particulars of observation, though those particulars may largely determine reliability. The plausibility of any theory is not, as we saw, limited to the reliability of the observations or data that are conjoined with the theory, but is determined by a host of other considerations that themselves make up a network of theory, prejudice, and observation. Thus, the plausibility of the Oedipal theory, which gives rise to the proposition that five-year-old boys should be jealous of their fathers, is not completely dependent on the behavior of five-year-olds, but is the outcome of a large and indeterminant body of facts, facts in the sense above. So we should accept or reject a particular fact—the fact, for example, about the jealousy of five-year-olds—not simply on the basis of observation (direct observation would be a very poor tool for the rejection of this fact, as psychoanalytic theory testifies), but on the coherence of the entire theory. Or, to take an even more radical example, the scientific status of extrasensory perception depends not on its factual status so much as on its status in a whole coherent body of science from psychology to physics. Scientists are not skeptical about extrasensory perception so much because they think the data are poor in ESP experiments, as because they are loath to give up an enormous complex of theory and data that would be challenged by uncritical acceptance of ESP as fact. Thus, when we say that this or that is a fact within the framework of a theory, what we mean is that the factual status of that observation depends entirely on the adequacy of the theory. The adequacy of the theory, in turn, depends on a whole complicated structure of theory and observation.

In this sense, facts change historically. This should by no means be troublesome. At one time it was a genetic fact that an offspring represented a merging of the characteristics of the two parents. This is a fact that is in accordance with common observation. Children generally appear to be a blend of their parents, and that blend would be passed on to succeeding generations. Mendelian theory, however, argued that the heredity units must be separate and independent. When it became necessary to accept Mendelian theory, it was no longer factual to describe offspring as being a blend of the two parents. Rather, a factual description of the hereditary characteristics of the offspring was to say that the offspring exhibited unit characteristics received from both parents that could be separated again in later generations. Thus, a particular fact may change as a whole scientific structure changes.

If we regard the function of science as the gathering and stating of facts of this sort, then there are two problems in science. One is the reliability and significance of the observations related to the facts; the other is the generality of the theory. A general theory, of which there are few in psychology, is one in which the explicit derivation of a very large number of facts is possible. In a theory sufficiently detailed and powerful to give rise to a number of facts, some facts inevitably will be challenged. Questioning what we accept as fact is the function of empirical investigation in science.

4
THE PLURALISM
OF MODERN
PSYCHOLOGY

Psychology is a patchwork alliance of very different intellectual enterprises. Indeed, psychological problems are so varied that it is a question as to whether there *is* such a thing as a single discipline of psychology. The investigation of human personality and the investigation of the function of the lower brain centers in the rat clearly require radically different techniques and draw on widely varying traditions. The attitudes, the techniques, scientific and otherwise, and the standards by which results are judged vary so much from problem to problem in psychology that some psychologists have more in common with biologists than with colleagues in their own department, who may in turn have closer intellectual ties with sociologists. Students of introductory psychology reveal their concern about this matter when they complain that the course is a fragmented, unassimilated hodgepodge.

Experimental psychology

Experimental psychology is a central method of psychology that is applied in many fields. It is what its name implies, the investigation of psychological phenomena—behavior, in the modern context—by the use of experimental techniques. It depends on that

74

view in science that elevates the experiment to the most exalted position among the techniques of empirical data gathering. That elevation derives from the fact that the experiment makes causative inferences more plausible than does any other kind of investigation. The experimental psychologist, more than any other psychologist, has adopted the point of view of the scientist at large about causation and inference of causation. He believes experimentation to be superior to all other forms of investigation, and he has been something of an imperialist in an effort to convert the whole of psychology to this view.

Experimentation has always been of greatest use in those psychological problems in which physical variables dominate. Physical variables are of supreme importance in the study of sensation and perception, for investigations of these functions concern the impact that the physical world has on the organism. The very name for this study of sensation and perception—*psychophysics*—implies the interweaving of psychological and physical events. Psychophysics and the psychophysical methods began with the nineteenth-century German physicist G. T. Fechner, who devised a theory and experimental methods for studying the relationship between what he called the inner world (the mind) and the outer world (the physical world). With the demise of the concept of mind and the rise of behaviorism, psychophysics lost the metaphysical cast given to it by Fechner, but the basic methods and techniques outlined in great detail by him remained virtually unchallenged until very recently. Some new ideas arising from the application of aspects of general theory in the detection of signals have begun to supplant classical psychophysics, and Fechner's ideas about how to measure sensations have been supplanted by others. But the whole purpose of both classical psychophysics and modern signal detection theory is to provide ways of studying the precise relation between the ability of an organism to respond to a signal and the physical nature of that signal. The study of sensation, therefore, is the most representative field in experimental psychology. It would be foolish to suppose that much could be added to what we know about color vision by observing how people react to colors through opinion poll methods. We have reached the point where the accumulation of new information about color vision requires elaborate instrumentation, precise laboratory control, and highly sophisticated mathematical theory.

Another area in psychology in which experimentation is of particular importance is *physiological psychology*. Because the fundamental controls for many problems in physiological psychology do not at this stage of development demand the conceptual framework of physics that the study of psychophysics does, the physiological psychology laboratory is not conceptually physical in the same way that the psychophysical laboratory is. But the physiological psychologist does depend on his ability to change events in the laboratory, and thus his laboratory is physical in the ordinary meaning of the word. It requires a certain amont of mechanical and chemical intervention.

The events with which the physiological psychologist is concerned have to do with the relations between behavior and the structure of organisms. One of the classical techniques in the study of the function of the central nervous system embodies this relation. It consists of the removal of a portion of the brain and then a comparison, based on some psychological function, of the effects of that removal with a control condition. This is an obvious example of the physical things that can be done to an organism. Portions of the nervous system can be altered or removed or the organism can be injected with chemically active substances, and the effects of these can be observed in controlled experimental settings.

Physiological psychology owes its methodological stance and attitudes more to its relations with physiology than to anything else. Because the physiological psychologist has been heavily influenced by the physiologist, his attitude toward experimentation is apt to be somewhat different from that of a psychophysicist. The psychophysicist takes the stance that precise control, mathematical analysis of data, and the application of statistical treatment are of central importance. The physiological psychologist is apt to argue, on the other hand, that the demonstration of some phenomenon in a few cases or even in a single instance is sufficient to prove the case. The single-case argument does not appeal to more statistically oriented experimental psychologists. In recent years, physiological psychologists have been under pressure to use statistical techniques in the evaluation of the inferences they draw from experiments (although certain experimental psychologists, under the influence of the radical empiricism of B. F. Skinner, have expressed skepticism about statistical treatment). But this difference between physiological psychologists and students of sensation and perception is a minor one. All agree on the need for laboratory investigation, precise physical control of relevant events, and experimental comparison. This underlying agreement is manifested superficially in the fact that the laboratories of both the psychophysicist and the physiological psychologist are cluttered with physical instruments used for the control of stimuli and the recording of data.

Prompted by the success of the application of experimentalism to sensation and perception, experimental psychologists branched out into other fields. The first among these was the study of learning and memory. Hermann v. Ebbinghaus published the first empirical study of memory by experimental means in 1885. His greatest achievement was to discover that memory and learning could be studied by experimental techniques. But the investigation of memory in the tradition begun by Ebbinghaus requires a subtle but fundamental change in the notion of experimentation: variables are no longer physical. The number of conditions of importance to learning and memory that can be controlled in the traditional physical sense is surprisingly small. The time that it takes to present something, the number of things that can be presented to learn, and the number of repetitions imposed on the learner very nearly exhaust the list of such conditions. Although Ebbinghaus went way beyond them, these variables undoubtedly have assumed far more importance in the study of human learning than they would have if the study of learning had developed outside the experimental tradition. There are literally thousands of experiments in which the time of presentation of items to be learned or the time between items or trials is the object of study. These investigations often do not have much meaning, but experimenters repeatedly come back to them because they concern the only obvious physical variables that have any conceivable cognitive or intellectual significance.

Some psychologists would hold that many other kinds of conditions have been studied in human learning. That is true, but these conditions are not, in the ordinary sense, physical changes, nor are they, in the ordinary sense, conditions that can be controlled by experimental operation. Instead, these variables are correlated with so-called response variables. They are, in effect, psychological conditions, which must be evaluated by obtaining responses from people. An enormous number of investigations, for example, have been aimed at studying *meaningfulness*. "Meaningfulness" does not mean to the experimental psychologist what it does to the layman. In the technical sense used by students of verbal learning, it is a single concept for describing a numer of aspects of verbal material. These aspects include the number of associations that a particular word can produce in a person over a fixed period of time, whether or not an associate occurs to such a word at all, a rating of the familiarity of those words, the ease of pronouncing those words, and whether the words are real words or nonsense words. All of these aspects of words and syllables are correlated, and learning about them depends on getting people to react to verbal items. They are ways of finding out how we react to words. Words that we find it easy to give associations to are also words that are familiar and easy to pronounce; hence, there is a certain logic to summarizing these things by a single concept of meaningfulness.

The basic strategy in research on meaningfulness consists of a ·study of the correlation (though the familiar correlation coefficient itself is not always used) between these variables and measures of performance in various rote verbal learning situations. The authors of these investigations often regard such studies as experimental, but they are experimental only in the sense that the investigations occur in a particular setting in a psychological laboratory. The variables that are said to control performance in these learning situations are *themselves* measures of performance. For example, some studies are concerned with the relation between familiarity with words and ease of learning. In order to assess familiarity, psychologists ask subjects to rate the familiarity of words. Another group of individuals will then be asked to learn combinations of these same words by some rote verbal learning technique. The ease of learning particular words on the part of one group of subjects is correlated with the rating of familiarity obtained from another group. This kind of research is correlational and not truly experimental. Like all such research, the inferences that can be drawn from it are limited by the logic of covariation. Such limitation is inherent in almost every empirical investigation in the field of verbal learning, and it characterizes almost all the studies of any real significance. These remarks are not intended to be critical. It is simply a fact that students of verbal behavior can make only limited use of the traditional notion of experimentation as that notion is derived from the physical model.

The extension to social psychology and personality

Experimentation has also been applied to social psychology and the study of personality. But, as we have seen, the superficial application of the ideal physical control in these conditions misses an important point. Social psychological events are mediated by the conditions in the minds of people. These, in turn, are determined by the past history of those individuals and by their perception of the social situation in question. Thus, to say that one "controls" a social psychological situation by the introduction of some condition sponsored by the investigator—the presence of a confederate of the experimenter, for example—is not entirely accurate. It is true that such an event (the presence of the confederate) may be reproducible and at the independent bidding of the experimenter, but it is also true that the significance of that event is psychological, not physical, and is dependent on the interpretation given it by the subject in such an experiment. Thus, the independent variable of the social psychologist bears only a superficial resemblance to that of the psychophysicist or physiological psychologist. The physiological psychologist can perform a physical action of considerable importance that in no way depends on interpretation by the subject of the experiment. He can, for example, remove the frontal lobe of an experimental animal. The removal of the frontal lobe will not depend on how the animal "sees" the situation, although it is conceivable that such might be the case in an experiment on human subjects. In fact, human experimental studies of psychophysiology are fraught with many of the difficulties inherent in social psychological experimenting. This has been evident in the whole conception of psychosomatic medicine and in the large number of studies that have investigated the psychophysiological reactions of human beings as determined by social conditions.[1] The essential fact is that control in an investigation in social psychology with an adult human being as subject depends on the interpretation that the person being studied places on the sequence of events in the laboratory. This makes experimental studies in social psychology or in the psychology of personality subtly but profoundly different from experimental studies of sensation or of brain mechanisms. In psychophysics, the stimuli have no social significance that requires interpretation.

The classical investigations that introduce the experimental method to the study of personality are those on psychological stress. In most of these experiments an individual is emotionally aroused by some technique. It is not so much the physical event that produces the stress as it is the interpretation that the individual being stressed places on that event. A given physical event may be only mildly stressful to one individual and extremely stressful to another; it depends on the individual's interpretation. Likewise, an innocuous physical situation may under certain circumstances be more stressful than an intensely noxious situation under other circumstances.

In short, in personality and social psychology (as well as in the study of verbal learning) the notion of experiment has undergone some metamorphosis from its original conception. Again, there is nothing to be criticized in these investigations in themselves. Experimental social psychology has made valuable contributions, and some investigators of psychological stress have insisted on the central role of interpretation of stressful events in the determination of the effects of stress.[2] Harm is done only when the

[1] By now there is a great deal of literature on this subject. Perhaps the best known reference is S. Schachter, "The Interaction of Cognitive and Physiological Determinants in Emotional States," in L. Berkowitz, ed., *Advances in Experimental Social Psychology*, Vol. 1 (New York: Academic Press, 1964).

[2] See R. S. Lazarus, *Psychological Stress and the Coping Pattern* (New York: McGraw-Hill, 1966).

investigator takes a simplistic view of the nature of the investigation, borrowed from the classical conception of the experiment. We must realize that the full inferential power of the classical. experimental method is not available in most social psychological experiments. Perhaps the truly important results of such experiments are not in the behavior but in what runs through the subject's mind during the course of the experiment.

Developmental psychology

Some areas of psychology have until quite recently been almost entirely free of the pressure to cast research in the model of the classical experiment. One of these is developmental psychology. Developmental psychology had its beginnings in the tradition of natural observation. Early students of developmental psychology were mainly concerned with producing age-graded norms of behavior. These norms were widely used, and to a large extent, they still characterize the field to the layman. In recent years the normative approach has been supplanted by studies arising out of theories of human development that have come chiefly from the work of Jean Piaget. The ideas of Piaget (and to a lesser extent, psychoanalytic notions) have been responsible for the introduction of quasi-experimental situations comparable to the kinds of experiments now commonplace in social psychology.

A moment's reflection should reveal to anyone who has taken a psychological test that such a test has some of the characteristics of an experiment. The test is a specially devised situation for the purpose of making some scientific observation. The observation is not completely at the mercy of chance events, as it would be under natural conditions, but is determined by the constraints introduced by the testing situation. There are elaborate directions for most psychological tests, and sometimes tests require special apparatus. Test standardization provides a kind of uniformity that makes it possible to compare the test results from one person with those from another. Developmental psychologists were among the first to discover that in order to compare different kinds of people, it would be necessary to use standardized testing situations. Hence, developmental psychology and the psychology of individual differences have always been closely related. By standardizing the testing situation it is possible to compare one individual with another. The effects of environmental events on development can be investigated by such comparisons. Such studies are of particular importance in questions about the interaction of biological factors with experience in development. There is, then, a kind of continuity between ordinary psychological testing and the type of investigation that draws on the classical model of the experiment.

An interesting example of the experimental method in developmental psychology is provided by a study of the smiling response. Children between the ages of five and six weeks and about four or five months will generally smile when stimulated by something corresponding to the human face. Most parents discover this sooner or later. During early infancy the baby is indifferent as to who plays with him. The baby will smile at his mother, but he will also smile at his grandmother, at his father, even at a total stranger who leans over the crib and makes cooing noises. Later the infant becomes more selective. A strange face is apt to be frightening to a six-month-old infant. The period during which the child will smile at many human beings is an interesting one, and because of its possible implications for socialization, it has been intensively studied by psychologists. It turns out that the essential feature that causes smiling is not, as most adults suppose, the cooing noises. Rather it is the motion made by the face bobbing up and down in front of the baby. This conclusion comes from comparisons of the various kinds of situations that will produce smiling in infants.[3] The cooing noises help, but the critical stimulus is the full view of a face in motion. A face in profile is not nearly as effective. And it does not have to be a human face, but simply something that displays the schematic characteristics of the human face. Babies will smile at a grotesque Halloween mask or at a crude caricature of the human face painted on a paper bag.

These facts came from the introduction of quasi-experimental variations into the study of infant development. Because the young

---

[3] The classical work on this aspect on infant socialization is that of R. A. Spitz, "The Smiling Response: A Contribution to the Ontogenesis of Social Relations," *Genetic Psychology Monographs*, 1964, 34, 57–125.

infant lacks the linguistic means for conceptualizing his world, he is much more like an animal than a socialized human being in an experimental situation. The infant mind places little interpretation on events. Thus, we may make inferences with reasonable plausibility about the way in which an infant reacts to stimulation in the smiling response stage. The way in which a five-year-old might react to a Halloween mask bobbing up and down at the foot of his bed is another matter.

It can be argued, of course, that the problems of developmental psychology are nothing more than the problems of psychology as a whole, for developmental psychology encompasses nearly all the special fields of psychology. There are developmental studies of the senses as well as developmental studies of language, emotion, and motivation. But a special property of developmental psychology is that it evaluates and compares the psychological processes of individuals at different ages. It is dominated by the notion that there is some orderly progression in psychological development, a progression that in part reflects original human nature and in part reflects the influence of experience on the developing child. It is the special problem of developmental psychology to discover the general principles that govern this progression and why it operates in the way it does. To the investigation of this problem, psychologists bring not only the methods that are familiar in other aspects of psychology but also a special comparative method uniquely appropriate to the area. In the comparative method the problem is to identify common themes that run through what appear to be quite different observations.

The most significant contemporary theory of intellectual development comes from the work of the Swiss psychologist Jean Piaget. Many psychologists, however, have criticized Piaget for the looseness of his observations and for his tendency to report observations colored by some theoretical presupposition. To a certain extent these criticisms are justified, although we should be aware by now that it is impossible for any set of scientific observations to be entirely free of the influence of preconception. Piaget, however, tries so hard to identify the underlying themes of human intellectual development that it is often difficult to determine the situation from which his observations are taken. Indeed, in some cases it is not certain that observations have been made at all, but the assumption of some underlying principle has resulted simply in the construction of an episode in development that might, if it had occurred, embody such a principle. Nevertheless, Piaget's theories have produced a whole new mass of important studies of development, many of which are distinguished by subtle and methodological sophistication.

One of the major features of nearly all theories of psychological development—including Piaget's—is that they emphasize saltatory changes. They characterize psychological development as going by fits and starts rather than smoothly. This has given rise to the notion of *stages* of development. During a stage, a particular underlying mechanism, such as the quality of intellectual function or motivation, remains relatively fixed and unchanged. The same stage may occur in different individuals at different times. Simply averaging together some quantitative results of observations would result in a continuous distribution of whatever is under investigation rather than a distribution by stages. For this reason, developmental psychologists have sometimes been cautious about statistical averages of data from individuals selected at random used to represent a particular chronological age. Their suspicions are justified if their ideas about stages of development are correct. But avoiding statistical averages has occasionally led the developmental psychologist into generalizing observations on a single case. More often, the developmental psychologist is apt to write as if a characteristic in an individual will emerge suddenly in a clear-cut way, when in fact for most individuals that characteristic may be complicated, determined by a number of different conditions, and thus may emerge gradually. The detection of stages is a principal problem in developmental psychology. A properly skeptical attitude on the part of the student should lead him to keep an open mind about the notion of stages until it is embedded in a sophisticated theory and rich empirical evidence.

The trouble with theoretical preconceptions in developmental studies is the assumption that a point of view is correct simply because it makes a sensible story. This is the problem of myth versus science. Even some highly developed and rigorous theories of developmental psychology require more data than they explain. A given theory may make a good story about how things got to be the way they are, but if it has little empirical content, it does not provide a plausible basis for action. Action in psychology—technological development or some therapeutic procedure—is often undertaken without any justification other than some appealing theoretical fancy. Whatever one thinks of psychoanalytic theory, one must admit that its therapeutic procedures are not as rigorously based as those that would lead us to apply a program of vaccination for smallpox. As long as developmental theories—such as those of Piaget, or more recently, those of psycholinguists—are not used to institute a massive change in education or treatment of children, perhaps the question of the empirical consequences of a theory is nothing more than academic. But if we try to design a particular kind of remedial linguistic training for children who have somehow missed the transition from one critical phase of linguistic development to another (according to a theory of development), we would be engaged in action. Then the question of whether the theory had much in the way of empirical consequences would be a real one. Unfortunately, a pressing social problem, such as that of trying to undo the deprivation of very poor children, has in some cases led to broad and expensive programs with little empirical justification.

Psychometrics

One of the most highly developed technologies in psychology is *psychometrics*. In fact, some psychometric theorists pride themselves on having no psychological content to their theories at all, so at least some aspects of psychometrics might be said to be exclusively a technology. Theories of psychometrics apply to the development of tests of ability and more recently tests of a variety of personality characteristics. The use of the tests is based on the application of a particular kind of statistical theory to the results of testing. The items in the test can be utterly independent of the psychological problem under investigation. Thus, the developers of one famous personality test, the Minnesota Multiphasic Personality Inventory (MMPI), argue that the content of the items that make up the test is, psychometrically speaking, irrelevant. What is important is that those items predict as efficiently as possible certain kinds of outcomes that have practical consequences. For example, one might administer the MMPI to find out if a young unmarried woman would be likely to become depressed after the birth of a child. The prediction would be based not on the content of the items on the test, but rather on whether or not the woman's responses agreed with those of other women who were known to have become depressed in the same situation. In short, the use of the MMPI is based on almost unalloyed empiricism. There are, in fact, no items in the MMPI that have anything to do with how people feel after childbirth. In theory, the items that make up the MMPI could range from the most trivial question, such as inquiring as to whether one puts one's right shoe on before one's left shoe, to matters of great psychological significance, such as whether or not one often thinks about suicide. The psychometrician could not care less about the content of items. Questions of great psychological significance have no more weight than do questions that appear to be superficial. What determines the presence of an item on a test of personality such as the MMPI is not the content of the item but simply the extent to which it predicts some criterion. We usually find out how well a given personality test predicts an outcome by means of the magnitude of the correlation between the test and the criterion.

Psychometric theory is not psychological in content; it is really a technology.[4] It does not contain statements and assumptions about the nature of the human mind or its relationship to its physical substrate; instead it makes assertions about doing things in such a way as to result in the most efficient outcome. While that kind of theory will not lead us to learn anything basic about the human mind, it may provide us with useful instruments for applying fundamental theory about the mind to actual observation. Occasionally psychometric theory is fruitfully wedded to psychological theory. The method of test construction known as construct valid-

---

[4] There has been an elaborate mathematical development of the statistical analysis that constitutes the body of psychometric theory. But the theory is not without problems. These problems have to do with the definitions of such theoretical entities as "true scores" and "error components" and their mathematical significance.

ity does this. And despite the way in which the Minnesota Multiphasic Personality Inventory, the California Personality Inventory (CPI), and other purely empirical inventories are constructed, some students of personality, genuinely concerned with the significance of particular items on such tests, are investigating the relations between the content of those items and the content of psychological theory. But we must recognize that psychometric theory in itself is not part and parcel of the main body of psychological theory. This fact is sometimes ignored in textbooks that treat psychometrics as if it were psychological. These books give the impression that the application of correlational studies of empirical validity can lead directly to some fundamental psychological truths. Such truths can be recovered only when the techniques of psychometrics are supplemented by more direct arguments about the nature and structure of psychological processes.

Individual psychology

Another radically different set of attitudes is associated with what has been, at various times, called individual psychology, ideographic psychology, humanistic psychology, and the psychology of character. Whatever the label, it is meant to describe the work of psychologists who attempt to study the richness of individual human life. Their method is essentially a case method. A person is explored in depth, by interview, life history, and perhaps through special assessment techniques such as projective tests, in which he supposedly "projects" his personality. The psychologist uses insights from literature, myth, drama, and the study of comparative culture to tease from the individual those aspects that would ordinarily be hidden from view. The attitude of the individual psychologist is often frankly and avowedly antiscientific. He is apt to be against scientific theories, experimental methods, statistics, and all the familiar tools of the typical psychologist. When pressed, he will seldom admit to being against knowledge. Thus, in the most general sense perhaps, he would object to being accused of being antiscientific. What he is really against is the *culture* of science.

There is much to be said for the attitude of individual or

humanistic psychologists, given many of the excess claims of the scientifically oriented psychologist, but the individual psychologist more often than not is also guilty of excess claims. And they are often as difficult to detect as the implicit assumptions of, say, experimental psychologists who try to fit a problem in social psychology to an inappropriate method of investigation. For one thing, the individual psychologist seldom has any reliable criterion of knowledge. If there is one important contribution of scientific psychology it is the requirement that knowledge about ourselves and our interpersonal relations be subjected to the same high standards of reliability that we associate with knowledge about the physical world. The individual or humanistic psychologist is apt to ignore these standards. He takes the view that knowledge comes from within, from intuition. It is not unfair to say that there is a strain of mysticism in the attitude of such psychologists.

Individual psychology is meant to lead to two kinds of knowledge: knowledge about particular individuals studied and knowledge about human nature in general. In the first respect the individual psychologist runs the risk of *creating* his character as much as studying him. The successful biographer is sometimes a good psychologist, and when he is, his work often verges on fiction. That is why traditional historians criticize psychological interpretations of historical figures. They are, almost intuitively, fiction and fantasy as much as they are history. In the second respect the individual psychologist runs the risk of creating as much myth as science. Psychoanalytic theorists are often individual psychologists, and the comments made earlier about myth in psychoanalytic theory apply to most varieties of individual psychology.

Perhaps it is fair to say that the individual psychologist trades reliability for freedom. It is, as we have seen, a characteristic of science that its ideas are constrained by nature. Science is not about everything; it is about empirical knowledge. The total freedom from constraints of any sort that characterizes the most radical of individual psychologists moves them out of the mainstream of science. Whether individual psychology gives rise to an art, or whether an art is possible without a science, is discussed in the next chapter.

Dynamic and structural investigation

From this discussion of the different types and methods of psychology, it should be apparent that the approaches to problems in psychology can be characterized by a number of different and sometimes contradictory attitudes. The experimentalist believes in pushing the methodological power of the experiment to—and perhaps beyond—its limits. The developmental psychologist stresses observation and the significance of long-term processes in human life. The psychometrician believes in the application of statistical technology to problems. The individual psychologist believes in the value of subjective experience in understanding the nature of the human mind. Such contrasting attitudes contribute to the highly differentiated nature of contemporary psychology. There are not simply two cultures in psychology, but many.

Nevertheless, a fundamental set of contrasting attitudes cuts across all the domains of psychology. It can be characterized by the polarity between dynamic and structural studies. Dynamic studies imply the examination of the causative relations among variables. For example, we may make the assumption that the object of study (a person) is under the influence of one or more motive forces and that these motive forces interact with one another in a way that causes sequences of actions. In structural studies the goal is more abstract and not influenced by the obsession with energy that characterized nineteenth-century physics. The goal is to describe relationships among the parts or components of a larger system. Traditional scientific psychology has been dynamic in character, despite the difficulties of conforming psychological subject matter to a dynamic scheme. There is considerable pressure both from psychology and the intellectual community at large to make social psychological studies and studies of human personality dynamic rather than structural. But, as some contemporary anthropologists and humanists have discovered, social events lend themselves more naturally to description than to the analysis of causes. In modern anthropology, explanatory principles of human action of a generation ago, based on psychoanalytic theory, have been largely replaced by the description of aspects of the social structure of a culture and how that social structure is reflected in the intellectual structure of individuals who make up the culture. For example, the interest in kinship and similar topics is generally not dynamic but structural.

There is evidence that sociologists are turning in much the same direction, although sociologists, under pressure for social application, are still heavily committed to dynamic conceptions. A great deal of current sociological research has been undertaken with policy decision as the goal (as, for example, various studies of the effects of segregated schooling in the United States). In the final analysis such studies are correlational (structural) in nature, and some sociologists are at last questioning the wisdom of trying to apply the structural techniques of correlational analysis to dynamic decisions about what causes what in such questions. We have been led to assume that the clearly demonstrated association between poor schooling and segregation of blacks can be eliminated by desegregating schools. In short, the association is regarded as a causative one, and one that acts blindly, irrespective of other factors. A structural investigation of the problem would examine the nature of education received by black students compared with that received by white students, and it would not make the assumption that desegregation would automatically provide better education for blacks, for it would make no strong causative inference.

At least some sociologists and some social psychologists are willing to accept the pattern of interrelationships exhibited by statistical analysis of social data as no more than just a pattern. They realize the enormous difficulty and perhaps impossibility of drawing causative inferences from the study of social institutions and social relations among men. At the same time, the importance of broadly conceived and detailed structural studies of society is testified to by the number of special institutes, centers, and organizations that do nothing more than watch society. Some of these do so for purely practical reasons. The demand for predictions about the use of goods or about the future of political candidates or advertising programs mingles in these analyses with the theoretical interests of the research scientist. Predictions that arise from survey studies, it should be noted, are usually strictly empirical bets (we guess that because 65 percent of the people are registered Democrats in 1968, the same proposition will hold in 1972). They are not based on plausible theories, and they are subject to all the blindness of pure empiricism.

The role of structural studies

The role of structural studies is to characterize in an efficient and understandable way the main characteristics of what is being studied. In social psychological studies the problem is to describe the fundamental nature of social relations among men. In studies of personality the primary structural problem is to characterize those features of an individual that are so important and enduring as to cause us to recognize him as a unique personality. The structural analysis of personality is usually a description of traits and types. Individuals are said to be characterized by certain fundamental features or attributes (traits), and various combinations of these attributes then (in some analyses, at least) describe types of individuals. But the types or traits may not exhibit themselves in all situations. Thus, traits may be highly context-sensitive. If such is generally the case, the psychology of personality is far more difficult than many of its practitioners would like to think. It is difficult, furthermore, to determine the difference between traits that are purely surface traits and those that are deep or fundamental. Psychologists have devised a number of special techniques to determine the structure of traits. In the traditional view personality inventories deal with surface traits. The deep or fundamental traits are to be found through projective tests.

Personality inventories and projective tests suffer from one psychometric limitation—their inherent unreliability. In the traditional view an item is said to be unreliable if there is a certain component of error in the reaction to the item. That is true no matter whether the item is on a personality inventory or a projective test. People are, for whatever reason, not supposed to react with perfect consistency to each item, and in psychometric theory, the inconsistency is essentially a random variable. To cancel un-reliabilities among items, test constructors add the results from test items together, just as does a third-grade spelling teacher, to arrive at a "score." The score on a test is usually a sum based on a number of the items (or more generally, some linear combination of items). The adding together of items is consistent with the psychometric notion that the context of items is unimportant. Almost no psychologist has challenged this view of reliability, despite the fact that it has become increasingly apparent that the method of test construction it engenders has reached the limits of its utility. Our tests are about as good as they can be, given our reliance on current psychometric theory. In order to divorce the study of personality from the theory of reliability as it exists in psychometric theory, a new conception of the structure of personality and ways to evaluate that structure are necessary. Otherwise, we must resign ourselves to marginal improvements on what we can do now.

In short, much of the fundamental study of personality within the framework of the traditional scientific view is empirical and relatively shallow. It is precisely this aspect that turns individual psychologists away from tests of personality. Scientific empiricism applied to personality has what validity it has as the result of the intuitions we derive from our knowledge of ourselves and one another. What the psychologist calls clinical insight determines the real content of our intellectual conceptions of the nature of human personality. The psychological study of personality, particularly in its more fundamental aspects, is shot through with superficial empiricism. There is almost no aspect of the study of personality for which there is satisfactory theory at present. For a number of years some psychologists thought that psychoanalytic theory, or perhaps some behavioristic translation of it, would serve as a framework on which to hang the whole of the psychology of personality. About thirty years ago at least some experimental psychologists thought that theories of learning might provide such a framework. These hopes have in large measure either disappeared or are simply reiterated in a kind of ritualistic way. The anti-intellectualism associated with extreme positions in individual psychology is no answer. This is simply a problem in psychology for which we have no inspiring solution at present.

Other divisions within psychology

The fields of psychology surveyed above are primarily the result of differences in attitudes toward method. The social psychologist, whose methodological allegiance is experimental, has more in common with the psychophysicist than he does with the structural anthropologist, who may be studying the same social psychological problem. Experimental psychology began with the study of the senses, and, as we have seen, was quickly extended to memory, thinking, and more recently, to personality development and social interaction. Psychometric theory originally arose in connection with the study of the development of human intelligence, but it has since been applied to an astounding range of psychological problems. The people applying these various methods often have difficulty communicating with the original students of the problem. It is a communication barrier based on method, not on subject matter, and there is no more serious aspect to the current crisis in psychology than this barrier based on method. Two books devoted to memory rest side by side on this writer's shelf. They might as well be about totally different subjects. One is by an experimental psychologist and the other by a clinical psychologist with a strong humanistic bent. It is very clear from their books that these authors could never effectively communicate with one another.

These methodological considerations provide the major structure for the field of psychology, but they do not provide the detailed division by subject matter. Division by subject corresponds, in the main, to the chapter titles found in introductory textbooks of psychology. Typically, there are chapters entitled *Learning, Intelligence, Emotion,* and so on. If the textbook makes some pretense to popularity and personal relevance, these may be disguised a bit by such phrases as *Effective Learning* or *Controlling Our Emotions,* but the same divisions are implied. These are topics of psychology. They reflect current fashion as well as history. Fashion changes more or less continuously—a once popular topic that has long since dropped out of favor is that of *Will* (although there is some evidence of a revival of interest in it). A topic that has had some vogue over the past twenty years but now gives evidence of waning interest is *Group Dynamics*. Despite the vagaries of fashion, the influence of history is strong. The special topics of psychology do not reflect an inherent or natural order in the phenomena of psychology; instead they reflect an accumulation of particular points of view.

There is a prejudice with strong historical roots to the effect that the mind, like Gaul, is divisible into three parts. The parts, ordinarily described as three kinds of mental functions, are *perception, cognition,* and *conation.* This division is a reflection of one of the most deeply embedded notions in Western psychology: intellectual functions are separate from emotion and motivation. This intellectual-emotional split pervades the whole of modern psychology. Almost no one—not the traditional experimental psychologist, the humanistic psychologist, nor the social psychologist— escapes it. Furthermore, it is a firm part of the folk psychology of our culture. According to both theology and common sense, man is supposed to have an intellectual-rational side and an emotional-irrational side. Yet there is nothing in the facts of psychology or even ordinary experience that makes such a dichotomy a necessity. On the contrary, one can make a good case for quite a different dichotomy. For example, there is at least some reason for supporting the hypothesis that intellectual processes that are linguistic are in their fundamental nature different from those that are nonlinguistic, and that many intellectual processes are at bottom governed by the same schemata that govern emotion.

In any event, the student of psychology should know that the topics reflected in the chapter headings of his textbook do not reflect the necessary and inevitable order of things. The facts of psychology, as we have seen, depend on psychological theory— explicit or implicit. No factual statement can be free of all preconception. So the fact that emotion and intellect are separate is a result as much of a certain way of looking at things as it is of nature itself. So it is with all the divisions in the special fields of psychology. There is not just one way of studying the nature of man, and it is an historical accident that one particular group of methods for studying man and the particular conception of mind that we think of as the only one in the late twentieth century is dominant now. Those of us who live and learn by the culture of our times know no other culture, and we must accept the facts of the world as they are determined not only by the observations of scientists but by the culture in which those scientists live. It is a cultural fact today that there are some scientists who call themselves psychologists and that these psychologists have developed a body of theory—both formal and informal—and a body of methods for investigating a conception called mind (or a version of that conception labeled behavior). An awareness of the possibility of other ways of doing much the same thing is the key to progress in a scientific field, and the student who embarks on a study of psychology can do both himself and the field a service by keeping that in mind.

5
PSYCHOLOGY TODAY AND TOMORROW

Psychology in America, almost from the time it arrived as one of the new sciences from the universities of Germany, has been both theoretical and practical. The major concern in this account of psychology as science and art has been with the theoretical aspects, for the practice of psychology and the arts associated with it depend both directly and indirectly on psychology as a science. The psychological arts depend directly on scientific knowledge to the extent that they derive from such knowledge. And the practice of psychology depends indirectly on science because its acceptance by society at large results in no small measure from the prestige and intellectual significance attached to the idea of scientific psychology.

The one thing that really sets late twentieth-century American psychology apart from late nineteenth-century American psychology is the magnitude of the enterprise. From modest beginnings, the discipline of psychology has become one of the dominant influences in American culture. *Psychology Today*, founded a few years ago, is now a mass circulation magazine with great influence among the upper middle and managerial classes of the country. Its very existence testifies to the enormous growth in scientific psychology since the time of William James. The results of scientific investigation in psychology are felt in all human activities, from medicine and the health sciences to corporate management and the problem of coping with the *anomie* and alienation that seem to be the consequence of life in an overdeveloped mass economy. Modern psychology is a science, although as we have seen, that science is liberally mixed with myth and magic. To a certain extent, the doctrines, facts, and prejudices of modern psychology have come to replace religion, faith, and the morals of natural law for many people. This kind of social influence makes it doubly important that we become aware of the way in which science and myth are almost inextricably mixed in contemporary psychology. In earlier chapters we examined the methods and views that gave rise to this mixture. In this chapter, we shall survey that mixture in the dominant themes of contemporary psychology, themes with the power to tell us what direction psychology will take in the future. The first of these themes is a recent revival—the notion of mind and its curious coexistence with the powerful streak of behaviorism in American psychology, a streak that has now become worldwide.

The revival of mind

Our present idea of the nature of mind cannot be grasped without an understanding of the mind-matter or, as it is sometimes expressed, nature-soul dichotomy. That dichotomy, known generally as psychophysical dualism, has existed in Western thought for at least two thousand years and perhaps from the very beginning of Greek speculative philosophy.[1] Psychophysical dualism asserts that the universe is made of two entirely separate modes of being, matter and mind. René Descartes, the seventeenth-century French philosopher, gave that notion its best-known modern version; he insisted that mind and matter could mutually influence each other. German philosophers of the seventeenth and eighteenth centuries argued that psychophysical interactionism, as Descartes' doctrine was called, was illogical; they were more inclined to the

[1] J. R. Kantor has maintained for a number of years now that dualism arose from the intellectual contamination of Greek objectivity by oriental, chiefly Persian, philosophies as the result of the spread of Christianity. See J. R. Kantor, *The Evolution of Scientific Psychology*, Vol. 1 (Chicago: Principia Press, 1963).

view known as psychophysical parallelism, which asserts that mind and matter coexist but do not interact or influence each other. This is a more fastidious view because it permits the absolute separation of the physical sciences from the psychological sciences. Physics in this view is the science of matter and energy while psychology is the science of mind and will. That dichotomy grants a certain grand stature to psychology. Psychology becomes the equal of physics in the partitioning of the domain of knowledge, if not in methodological sophistication and degree of abstractness. When Darwinian theory, the growth of biology, and the rise of behaviorism began to discredit the notion of psychophysical dualism, psychology lost its royal status. Behavior, like everything else, is basically physical in nature. If there is no special mode of existence called mind, then psychology has no unique and inviolable subject matter. It is simply a branch of biology, and in the view of the logical positivists, biology is simply a branch of physics.

Thus, the behavioristic revolution robbed psychology of its special intellectual domain. Psychology has since become more practical and of more interest to thinkers as well as ordinary folk, but in the grand view of things it was no longer the guardian of a unique entity—mind. As the notion of mind began to disappear in the intellectual-scientific world, the parallel notion of soul in religion and philosophies that have their origin in religion likewise began to disappear, or at least to undergo drastic transformation. The immortality of the soul is no longer central in the writings of contemporary Christian theologians, and Jewish theologians can remind them that it never was an essential part of Judaism. In a sense, the soul became behavioristic too.

Yet, in the past ten years there has been a revival of the notion of mind. Textbooks of twenty years ago asserted that psychology was the science of behavior. They now say that psychology is the science of behavior *and mind*, and one text, published a few years ago, unashamedly carries the title, *Psychology, The Science of Mental Life*. Does this mean that modern psychology has returned to the main tradition of Western dualism? Probably not, for the revived notion of mind is radically different from the one implied by the grand psychophysical dichotomy. Psychologists are still hostile, in the main, to dualism, and even when they are not, the implications of the dualistic view remain largely unexplored. The emphasis in contemporary psychology is on the mind as a part of the physical universe. But the increased tendency to use the term "mind" is not simply an idle terminological reversion. It reflects a genuine intellectual change. In part it reflects the realization that behavior is only the outward manifestation of what really counts. In part it also reflects a belief, not fully articulated, that an organization as complicated as man's central nervous system, together with its relations with other organs and systems, gives rise to emergent phenomena that may be unique in the world. An emergent phenomenon is something that is not predictable or understandable from the properties of the components taken individually and independently. The central nervous system of man, embedded in its biological context, gives rise to phenomena that simply are not understandable from a knowledge of the physical properties of the individual nerve cells that compose it. Consciousness, the continuity and organization of perception, memory, language, and the feeling of knowing and willing are all emergent phenomena that arise from the organization of the body's cells. Psychology, in the contemporary view, is the study of these emergent systems and the term "mind" is as good as any to describe them in totality.

In this way psychology has come into a new relation with the physical sciences. It is no longer one of the two imperious monarchs dividing the realm of knowledge, nor is it any longer simply an unimportant branch of physics in the hands of third-rate practitioners. It is instead the study of systems of organization that grow out of complex neural networks, themselves part of biological systems called organisms. These systems called mind have properties almost unknown in the rest of the universe, and these properties call for special modes of study. Modern computing machines are systems of organization that come closer than anything else to the systems called mind, and it is no accident that the revival of the notion of mind coincided with the development of computer sciences. There is a deep and significant relation between modern psychology and computer sciences. That relation is no less significant because there exists no computer like the human mind. Nor is there any reason for computer technologists to build such a computer other than in the interests of psychological research.

There are many kinds of systems, and they all have the property that the result of the relations of the parts is not inherent in the parts themselves. The principle of the lever, for example, is not inherent in a stick of wood or a block of wood, but the stick as lever and the block as fulcrum bring into existence a system that, in theory, is able to multiply applied force to an unlimited extent. The organization of the United States Congress is not in 535 men and women and some rules on paper. The intricate interactions of those who compose the Congress have brought a special social and political system into being. All the social sciences are sciences of systems, of relations among parts. Psychology has a unique place between those sciences dealing with biological systems and those that are purely social. The principles of systems organization should enable us to realize that the properties of mind cannot be determined from the individual biological components, and psychologists sometimes forget that social and economic organizations cannot be determined completely from knowledge of the nature of the individual human mind.

To say that the human mind is a system does not, of course, dispose of all important problems. The status of conscious experience remains a puzzle. A century ago it was possible to believe in a simple theory of the nature of consciousness. It was just the manifestation of that mode of existence known as mind; mind and consciousness were identical. But the discovery, in the late nineteenth century, of the significance of unconscious processes in human mental activity forever destroyed that view. Freud is the best-known discoverer of the importance of unconscious processes, but he was not the only one. A group of experimental psychologists associated with the University of Würzburg in Germany uncovered the role of unconscious processes in human intellectual activity; while less spectacular and less influential, their work is as profound as Freud's. Today we take it for granted that conscious experience presents merely the surface of human emotional and intellectual activity. But there is still no satisfactory account of why some activities are conscious while others are not. In fact, no clear idea of the nature of consciousness itself exists, although many psychologists, including those who have been heavily influenced by Freud and by psychoanalytic theory, assume that in some significant way it is connected with language. No problem presents a greater puzzle to psychology than the persistent question of the nature and function of consciousness.

Many aspects of the revival of the notion of mind have been beneficial. One is the kind of analysis that leads to the view of the mind as system. Another is the scientific respectability granted once more to such questions as those concerning the nature of conscious experience. A happy coincidence is the fact that this revival came along about the same time that the attention of psychologists was called to biochemical and other physical procedures that, in conjunction with little understood psychological and social conditions, produced altered states of consciousness. Many psychologists who had felt constrained by the rigid prohibitions of behaviorism can now turn their attention to such problems as the relation between drugs and conscious states, and the relation between electrical activity in the brain and states of consciousness.

The contemporary behaviorists

Despite the new respectability given to the term "mind" and the enlargement of the notion of system, a considerable segment of contemporary researchers in psychology view themselves as behaviorists and psychology as a behavioral science. They see the intellectual task of psychologists very much as Watson did, as the prediction and control of behavior. How, one might ask, can the behaviorists and the neomentalists both be right? Are not their views absolutely contradictory? In a certain sense, of course, they are, but in other ways it is quite possible for the behaviorist and the neomentalist to operate side by side, or even to engage in a somewhat uneasy cooperation. This is partly because each has as much a myth or point of view to offer as he does hard fact and technique. Behaviorism offers certain attitudes, methods, and procedures that allow behavioral psychologists to solve some problems within the limited framework of behaviorism that are both theoretical and practical in nature. These solutions do not satisfy everyone, but judged by the canons of behavioral psychology, they work. To a remarkable extent, today's applied psychology is committed to a behavioral attitude, and that fact lends to behavioral psychology more importance than it would otherwise have, given the general changes in intellectual fashion in the social sciences.

The most widely known application of behavioral techniques is in programed instruction. Programed instruction, at least as it was developed by B. F. Skinner, the most significant figure among contemporary behavioral psychologists, aims to program material in such a way that the student rarely fails to make the "correct" response during the course of learning, and he is given immediate reinforcement for correct responses. Actually, programed instruction depends less on the fundamental theory and attitudes of behaviorism than do certain other aspects of behavioral psychology. Psychologists who are uncomfortable with behavioral theory have no objections to programed instruction and often feel free to make use of it, although they may not agree with the aims of the programs inspired by Skinner's analysis of behavior.

Many nonbehavioral psychologists regard behavior therapy, another significant application of behavior theory, with genuine distaste. They see behavior therapy as an attempt to treat the superficial symptoms—those symptoms that are readily manifested in behavior—rather than the problems that cause the symptoms. Behavior theorists reply that the symptoms *are* the problem—they define the complaint that brings the individual to therapy in the first place.

There is a certain amount of mutual hostility among the advocates of different modes of practice of behavior therapy. In general, however, all behavior therapies attempt to treat the symptoms of personality disturbance or deviation by applying the techniques of experimental psychology used in the study and control of animal behavior. In fact, the experimental studies of behavior in laboratory animals have traditionally been aimed at providing experimental support for one or another aspect of behavior therapy. This has been characteristic of such investigation from the time of Pavlov to the present. The various methods that have worked for the control of the behavior of rats, pigeons, and rhesus monkeys, behavior therapists argue, should also work with autistic children, schizophrenics, neurotics, and alcoholics. The specific procedures used by behavior therapists range from desensitization, which is a technique for removing symptoms by methods derived from Pavlovian conditioning, to procedures for reinforcing desirable behavior through techniques urged by B. F. Skinner. Occasionally these methods will be supplemented by some special technique such as punishment, the use of drugs, or an assault directly on the central nervous system. Thus, a homosexual individual might be treated by being painfully stimulated or made nauseated while exposed to erotic homosexual material and by being exposed to erotic heterosexual material under more pleasant circumstances.

Behavior therapists make much of the hardheaded attitude that comes from a behavioristic point of view. They insist that techniques of inducing psychological change be subjected to evaluation, preferably experimental, and dropped or altered if they don't work in experimental situations. Some positive evidence supports the efficacy of behavior therapy, but that evidence is by no means universally accepted. Research on all kinds of psychotherapy is subject to the most difficult obstacles, and the possibility of applying strong inferences about causation to genuine problems in psychotherapeutic research is slim and perhaps nonexistent. Critics point to possible contamination of tests of behavior therapy by placebo effects.

Even if the behavioral therapists' claims of elimination of symptoms are accepted, there are still problems with behavior therapy. Critics of behavior therapy argue that removing symptoms does not really get at the basis of an emotional problem and, in fact, may produce more harm than good by replacing some innocuous symptom with one that is potentially dangerous. They also argue that symptoms may be easily repressed or altered without touching the anxiety, conflict, or motivation that gave rise to them. This is an extremely difficult, if not impossible, argument to counter, for in the last analysis it is based on the essential open-endedness of psychological events. The consequences of any deliberately produced physical event may be limited, both in theory and practice, to some closed system, but *all* consequences of a psychological change are not foreseeable, and hence psychological change must be regarded as capable of producing undesirable consequences. This difficulty plagues all research aimed at producing practical psychological results, of course, but it is more apparent in the research on behavior therapy because of the forthright, tough attitude toward the criteria of successful treatment advanced by the advocates of behavior therapy.

Let us take for granted that under some circumstances and with some methods, behavior therapy is successful in completely or partially removing certain symptoms. Whether or not such therapy can cope with problems of smoking, homosexuality, alcohol, or other habitual modes of action as well as has been claimed may be at issue, but that some alterations in attitudes, emotional attachments, and even motivation can occur is beyond doubt. This much may be admitted even by someone who considers the basic premises of behaviorism to be incorrect. The divergence of opinion comes at the deeper level of interpreting what occurs in behavior therapy, or in any form of behavioral management, for that matter. The behaviorally oriented psychologist attaches psychological significance to events external to the organism. Organisms are controlled, he argues, by rewards, aversive stimuli, deprivation, and other operations that alter motivation, and by various external signals. The thoroughgoing behaviorist will argue that the behavior of all organisms, including man, can be brought under complete control and be made precisely predictable solely through the operation of external controls.

Here the neomentalist disagrees. No matter how much influence he may grant to the behaviorist's devices of external control, he attaches the greater psychological significance to conditions within the organism, to the organization of mental systems, and to devices of internal control. The neomentalist is apt to point to the cybernetic or self-controlling machine, to the computer, or to other highly organized systems rather than to the reflex for his psychological model. The behaviorist, on the other hand, tends to regard the notion of internal control with suspicion.

He will equate it with freedom of will.[2] The whole notion of psychological freedom strikes the behaviorist as mystical, unscientific, and somehow having religious connotations. He will perhaps grant that self-controlling machines are possible, but he will insist that someone has to design control features into them. The behaviorist is inclined to look with disfavor on the analogy between computing machines and human beings.

The controversy cannot be resolved. More than an argument at a scientific level, it represents a clash of intellectual styles. Furthermore, these differences are probably unresolvable on any level, for they may well reflect whole patterns of personality as these are expressed in commitment to one or another scientific point of view. Most psychologists will regard a total commitment to behavioral engineering as at one and the same time quixotic and totalitarian. But this should not blind us to the fact that external events—rewards and punishments—do enter into the totality of events that, at any given time, determine both the content of mind and the pattern of behavior that a given individual is likely to exhibit. Behavioral techniques may not be the best of all possible methods for solving the problems they were designed to solve, but they are, in many cases, new and add to our techniques for social engineering. Programed instruction is not a universal cure for all the problems of education, and behavior therapy will not allow us to turn over all the mental hospitals to, say, organic food communes; but they sometimes work, and they deserve their place in modern society. The problem is, however, that the committed behavioral engineer is seldom assailed by doubts. He firmly believes that his is the voice of science and not myth. So long as the total point of view of the behaviorist does not cause us to cast up a model of man that is simple beyond reality and alarming in its potential for intellectual restriction, recognition of the techniques of behavioral control on their empirical merits will not cause us to lose the insight that comes from a structural view of the scientific method, from a sophisticated appreciation of the com-

---

[2] Skinner presents a critical analysis of the concept of freedom from the standpoint of objective behaviorism in B. F. Skinner, *Beyond Freedom and Dignity* (New York: Knopf, 1971).

plexity of man's mind, and from a skepticism about psychological cure-alls.

At the same time we must bear in mind the open-ended nature of the social psychological system. We cannot completely predict the consequences of any particular action or deliberately induced psychological or social changes. This open-endedness operates at all levels—from that of the individual human mind to the conditions governing national economies and great stable social institutions. The critics of behavior therapy are right in principle. Nothing we know enables us to tell for sure that if we eliminate nail-biting through behavior therapy we will not induce some other, perhaps undesirable, change. In any well-defined physical system, side effects simply do not occur. Side effects of experimentation or physical engineering occur only on the frontier of knowledge in the physical sciences, where the traditional relations cannot predict adequately to allow the conditions of the classical experiment to hold (see Chapter 2). Side effects do occur in biological systems; one reason the practice of medicine is an art as well as a science is that the diagnosing and the prescribing physician must be prepared to take the risk side effects entail. In complicated social and psychological systems they are a positive risk, since no one knows enough about these systems to say with complete confidence whether or not side effects are negligible in such things as, for example, subjecting a person to some drastic psychotherapeutic treatment. In short, the same features that make the psychological experiment only an imperfect analogy to the physical experiment operate to make behavioral engineering only an imperfect analogy to physical engineering. Even when no fundamental theory is at stake, as is still the case in certain areas of physical engineering and as many behavioral engineers readily agree is the case in psychology, the analogy is imperfect, because even though we may not be able to give a satisfactory account of the physical limits of a physical change, experience provides precedents of some precision; psychological changes are themselves so embedded in an ever changing context that we may wonder if a precedent exists. Certainly, behavior therapy applied to homosexuality in America in the 1970s would have very different side effects than it would in the 1920s, when the ideas behind behavior therapy first began to germinate.

The growth of the influence of psychology

One aspect of the future of psychology about which we can have no doubt whatever is that its influence will grow. This is not because psychology will necessarily find itself able to solve more and more of society's problems, or because some startling new discoveries are even now waiting in the wings, but simply because society has nowhere else to turn for guidance and direction than to the social sciences in general and psychology in particular. In the past half century, the social sciences have grown from marginal respectability in American society to positions of great power and influence. For one thing, they fill the vacuum left by the demise of older institutions and ideas. They have also grown because the complicated networks of modern society require ever more sophisticated and more highly generalized techniques of management. We have come to depend on scientific research in psychology and the art and judgment of psychologists for such things as the treatment of crime and punishment of criminals as well as the selection and training of managers for the great industrial complex that comprises the private sector of the American economy.

The deep belief in Western culture that society should be improved by aiming at certain goals has given an especially important status to the social sciences, for they are now regarded as the chief instruments for designing changes to bring these goals about.

In the process of giving advice about factual matters and about the ways of achieving certain goals, psychologists and other social scientists have been asked to advise on the goals themselves. In short, it has been impossible to keep values from intruding into the practical relations between the social sciences and society. Often these intrusions of values are not recognized for what they are simply because the values of the social scientist have become an integral part of our social belief systems. That criminals should be rehabilitated, if possible, would be doubted by few in American culture (although perhaps it would not be so universally accepted a notion in Saudi Arabia, which follows the law of the Koran for criminals). Rehabilitation as the objective of the penal system is in keeping with, and is an outgrowth of, nineteenth-century developments in Judeo-Christian ethics, but as the chief, if not only, object of the penal system it is a creation of twentieth-century psychology and sociology.

That the goals of society today include the reduction of social conflict, concern with personal adjustment at all levels of society, and belief that guilt and anxiety are bad is a reflection of the fact that this is the century of psychology. Religion and traditional values—the ethics of natural law—once were the main source for the rules by which we were supposed to live. A variety of events, including the rise of psychology itself, have conspired to produce a new set of rules—those governing social concern have become utilitarian and to some extent Marxist, while those governing personal concern have become hedonistic and centered in the nature of the living process itself, in self-improvement and personal progress, rather than in the distant goals of life. These new values make considerable demands on social resources. In order to bring about personal adjustment and to promote happy life styles, society provides therapists, counselors, social workers, psychiatrists, and a whole bureaucratic structure to administer their services. There is every reason to expect that over the next twenty-five years society will devote an even larger portion of its available resources to the support of these services, for the evidence is that the value system that supports them is becoming more widespread and more firmly established in all developed nations.

The influence of psychology has extended to other fields. The practice of medicine has become increasingly psychological and will continue to do so in the future. This growth is seen not just in the increasing role being given to the traditional psychological specialists in medicine—the psychiatrists—it is also reflected in an increasing awareness on the part of practicing physicians of the psychological functions they must serve. Medical research in pediatrics, for example, has become heavily psychological in nature, and the demands of society for drastic change in the lives of the children of the poor and of ghetto residents will no doubt accelerate movement in this direction.

Even the law and our conceptions of legal justice have been drawn into the revolution brought about by the application of psychological science and practice to the social order. The famous 1954 decision on desegregation by the United States Supreme Court emphasized that the judiciary now recognizes the ability of psychological scientists to discover, through empirical means, things that we could only guess about before. The unevenness in quality of the legal applications of psychology and the often contradictory ideas expressed by two or more psychologists when asked to comment on legal matters has not impeded the growing dependence of the legal profession on the social sciences. Many of the leading law schools have introduced aspects of the social sciences in their curricula and have appointed psychologists and sociologists to their faculties. Because there is a certain politically induced inertia in the law-making bodies themselves, they have not been so dependent on advice and opinion from psychologists and sociologists. To an increasing extent, however, psychologists and others now testify before committees of Congress and various state legislatures on psychological aspects of new legislation, and their testimony is heeded.

Part of the increasing dependence of society on the psychological sciences and psychological practice is the inevitable result of the increased institutionalization of life in a society that is highly industrialized and perhaps overpopulated as well. It is possible to manage a frontier settlement with little bureaucracy and no concern for the least costly and most effective way of doing things. It is impossible to run New York City in this way. The task of making a complex social system work from one day to the next requires an army of bureaucrats, of which at least the managerial component has been largely educated in the ethos of the social sciences. Our social system may not work well, but it works, and it is doubtful that such a system could survive outside the framework provided for it by contemporary, empirically oriented social sciences. In fact, this close connection between official social science, including psychology, and bureaucratic management, whether in government or in private enterprise, has been the occasion for some bitter criticism from those who regard the whole contemporary social system as dehumanizing and repressive. The political right has always criticized the social sciences and contemporary psychology, but now criticism comes also from the new left. New left spokesmen argue that the social sciences, as institutionalized knowledge about man and his society, are the tools of the ruling oligarchy and are of little genuine human value. A similar attitude within the profession of psychology itself has been responsible for the remarkable growth of an institutionalized reproach to traditional psychology in the form of the Association for Humanistic Psychology.

The social sciences, of course, are not responsible for those aspects of modern life that most of us find dreary, dehumanizing, and degrading. They are simply a part of Western society's wildly accelerating growth in economic worth, productivity, population, and knowledge. Social scientists, concerned with providing sane reflective knowledge, are themselves victims of the enterprise that finds it necessary to provide them with, on a relative scale at least, very handsome financial support as a way of hedging against future problems. The modern Luddites have an impossible dream for they cannot destroy the inhuman fabric of modern industrial society without destroying the means for supporting the hundreds of millions of lives that industrial society made possible.

The critics do have an important role to play, nevertheless, for the practitioners of the social sciences have become the creators of the new goals, morals, and esthetics of the modern world. If the critics do nothing else, they should make psychologists and sociologists aware that they are more than ethically neutral scientists; they are shapers of policy. In arguing that the findings of modern psychology are ethically and politically neutral, the social scientists are espousing a view that, to an extraordinary extent, has dominated the efforts of American society since the Second World War. After a sobering glance at his role in society, the modern psychological scientist should recall the limitations on his methods and on the conclusions that he draws from his work, and he should remember that his science is also, to a considerable extent, myth. He should be even more sobered by the knowledge that the influence and significance of the view he represents will continue to grow.

The future of psychology

What are the future directions of the science itself? Where will new techniques, innovations, theories, and insights come from? What areas of psychology will be exciting in the next decade or so, and which ones will slumber in a state of suspended animation? Modern students of the history and sociology of science tell us that science moves not in a smoothly accelerating path but rather by fits and starts. In particular, individual sciences seem to be dominated for periods of time by vast frameworks compounded from suddenly developed theoretical insights, a climate of opinion, and a host of empirical discoveries that stem from the theoretical insights.[3] Psychology is no exception, and a special field in psychology moves by fits and starts as exciting ideas bring in new talent, and new instruments and techniques make possible things that could not have been done yesterday. Achieving a balanced view of the current state of psychology and its place among the social and biological sciences is difficult enough; extrapolation to the future is even more difficult. It is worth the effort, however, for it gives us a standard against which to judge the future when it comes.

The easiest way to explore the future of psychology is to try to figure out which of the fields of psychology is ripe for some new theoretical insight. Important theoretical insights, historians of science tell us, often serve to stabilize some scientific field for a number of years. For examples of this they nearly always point to physics. But theoretical insights are not common in psychology, or at least not as common as in physics. Revolutions in fields other than physics are slower, more diffuse, and probably more empirical. Thus, an empirical discovery, such as Pavlov's discovery of the conditioned responses, is as much a revolutionary event in psychol-

---

[3] This general view has its best-known exposition in T. Kuhn, *The Structure of Scientific Revolutions,* 2nd ed. (Chicago: University of Chicago Press, 1970).

ogy as is a formal abstract theory. The effect of theories in the social sciences and in biology is apt to be more diffuse because these theories have less explicit implications for research than do theories in the physical sciences. A new theory in physics generally makes quite explicit statements, leading to things that can be investigated in the laboratory. The actual investigation may have to await development of a new technology, but any delay is seldom because other scientists do not initially see the implications of the theory. In biology, at least until quite recently, new theories were less explicit. Darwin's conception of the development of species was revolutionary, but many of its most important implications were hidden and developed only slowly. Events that make sweeping and significant changes in psychology are even less clear-cut and more difficult to detect than they are in biology.

Some episodes in the history of psychology have had consequences that can be called revolutionary. The most important one thus far was the mid-nineteenth-century discovery that empirical research itself was possible in psychology. Another was the almost simultaneous and mutually supportive work of Pavlov on the conditioned reflex and of Watson on the fundamental notions of behaviorism. Still another was Freud's invention of psychoanalysis and his far-reaching discovery of the importance of unconscious phenomena. In recent years, it is probably fair to point to Skinner's discovery of the possibilities of behavioral engineering and, on the other side, to Chomsky's discovery that the remarkable properties of human language demanded a much richer view of the nature of the human mind than any purely behavioral theory could produce. Are there any other such events in the wings?

Certainly, if any field needs a revolutionary discovery, it is psychometrics, or research in the measurement of human abilities. We make practical use of both tests of ability and objective tests of personality, but there is no really satisfactory theory that tells us why such tests work, or the extent to which they are determined by inherent, genetic factors rather than by the accidents of individual experience. Many psychologists believe we need to approach the problem of mental measurement from a radically different standpoint. We have pushed our current ways of making and analyzing tests about as far as we can, and any real insight will probably require something very different. It is one thing, however, for a field, such as psychometrics, to be in need of a new insight and quite another to provide it. Many fields must remain fallow a long time before they are ready to be productive again.

Another area in psychology in need of new insight is human motivation. Freud, of course, was responsible for a radical new theory of human motivation, the consequences of which are still with us. Freudian views still dominate theories of human motivation largely because they are about the most highly developed ideas available. But there is some evidence that the Freudian well has run dry. Thirty years ago, it was responsible for new notions in anthropology as well as a host of special fields in psychology. For example, the so-called projective tests—the Rorschach Inkblot Test and the Thematic Apperception Test—were developed as a direct consequence of Freud's theory of motivation. One of the implications of his theory was that unconscious motivation is expressed in fantasy and in responses to unstructured, "meaningless" stimuli; hence the attempt to explore the personality by having people tell what they see in some abstract forms, such as those created by blotting ink on paper. The use of projective tests is currently in decline, and other similar implications of classical psychoanalytic theory seem to be less and less appealing. Building on Freud's shoulders, we can now see too far. We can see what is wrong with the older concept, and we clearly need something to replace it. Although there have been several attempts over the years, nothing thus far has been radical enough to give us an appreciably better understanding than that derived from a refinement of the notions of Freud.

Physiological psychology and related fields have developed more nearly like the layman's traditional view of the growth of science—as a steady increment in new empirical knowledge. Important discoveries have come from experimentation rather than theory, and they have been effectively buried in the context of continuous development. Several discoveries, of course, stand out. One is the discovery, in the mid-nineteen fifties, of the rewarding and punishing effects of direct electrical stimulation of certain portions of the brain. Hans Berger's discovery of so-called brain waves, or electroencephalogram, is another landmark. But even these dramatic empirical discoveries depend on the earlier work. They build on it rather than reject it. Discovery of the brain-stimulation effects, for example, depended on the invention by the Swiss neurologist W. R. Hess of techniques for exploring the interior of brains.

A profoundly important theoretical development that has seemed to be on the verge of happening in the last two decades is the discovery of the physical basis of learning and memory. Nearly all students of the physiology of learning and memory have argued that memory must have something to do with the configuration of molecules on the surface membrane of nerve cells. Just precisely what kind of molecules they are and how they may be altered to code information have eluded investigators. It is commonly assumed, however, that the coding and transmission of genetic information—by now fairly well understood—must provide an analogy to the storage of learned information on nerve cells. Perhaps so, but the possibilities remain just that; they are not even probabilities. The hazards of predicting the future are many —perhaps the real key to the understanding of human memory lies in the traditional empirically oriented work of physiological psychologists and not in the attempt to construct a theory of how memory could operate by analogy to genetic coding.

More than any other area in psychology, physiological psychology depends on and responds to discoveries in other sciences. Like biophysics it takes its life from the technologies made available by other sciences. It is critically dependent on anatomy and histology. Biochemistry and pharmacology provide an important contemporary source for experimental techniques. It is one of those curious accidents of intellectual history that the theoretical developments in biochemistry of significance to psychology came at about the same time that there was a widespread rebirth of popular interest in psychologically active drugs and a revival of psychological interest in states of consciousness and their alterations. The effects on psychological research of the convergence of these interests have not yet run their course, and it is possible that they may yet lead to another revolution in psychology.

What about extrasensory perception, mental telepathy, and other things traditionally grouped under psychic phenomena? Are we about to discover something mysterious behind mental manifestations? It is, by way of understatement, unlikely. The existence of mental phenomena totally independent of an underlying physical basis would upset not only current psychological notions but traditional physical notions as well. It would, for example, deny the universal validity of one of the greatest triumphs of nineteenth-century science, the laws of thermodynamics. Physicists are not worried. Truly revolutionary revisions in basic physical principles are always preceded by the rapid accumulation of incontrovertible evidence for a phenomenon that could not be explained by existing theory. In the few years preceding the discovery of X-rays, for example, all sorts of experimental facts testified to the inadequacy of the then current theories as to the nature of matter. Serious investigation of psychic phenomena is now nearly one hundred years old. Yet in that one hundred years and after thousands of experiments, no one has come up with a stable, repeatable phenomenon that would testify to mental events operating independently of physical systems. There is nothing remotely like the accumulation, in the last quarter of the nineteenth century, of evidence that classical physics did not work. ESP is a will-o'-the-wisp effect. Sometimes laboratory investigations come up with "statistically significant effects," but students of ESP are like dedicated gamblers—they lose what they gain. Perhaps the most important information to come from years of investigation of ESP is that processes we expect to be random, such as the coincidence of pictures on cards and people's guesses as to what those pictures are, are not quite random. In any event, psychologists and physicists are not ready to scrap the totality of the modern culture of science because they think there is strong evidence for psychic phenomena, nor does anyone but a handful of serious investigators think that the probability of something turning up is high enough to warrant making a career of investigating it. The possibility of a revolutionary change coming from this line of activity is small.

Recent developments in social anthropology, linguistics, and related social sciences have begun to have an influence in psychology. Psychologists have borrowed the concept of participant-observer studies from sociology and anthropology and put it to good use. And psychology has borrowed theory from linguistics. Perhaps the most important aspect of all this activity is that it is interdisciplinary. The traditional barriers among the social sciences seem to be loosening a bit. It is no longer unusual to find a psychologist doing phonetic studies, or a linguist engaged in experimental studies of language learning. The boundaries between the various social sciences are, to a considerable extent, arbitrary anyway. They depend on the traditions and skills acquired by different kinds of professional social scientists more than they do on the logic of dividing the problems of man and society for study. In the recent cross-fertilization, traditional ways of doing things that have nearly exhausted their usefulness within a particular discipline are put into service with new problems. The political scientists' recent discovery of statistics and psychological measurement has had a considerable influence on political theory. The notions of the great French anthropologist C. Lévi-Strauss have been influential in both the humanities and the social sciences. The spread of the ideas of Lévi-Strauss and those of the child psychologist Jean Piaget have been part of a process, almost unthinkable twenty years ago, by which the barriers between the humanities and the social sciences have been diminished.

Perhaps the most likely change for psychology in the future is a gradual redefinition of its subject matter, methods, and practice that will make it both broader in scope and less inhibited by tradition. At the same time, the functioning skills of particular psychologists will become narrower. This is inevitable in a discipline whose boundaries are being extended. Thus fields of psychology will grow and become independent disciplines in their own right, and new hybrid fields will be established on the borders. It is very clear that the practice of psychology, particularly the practice of clinical psychology, is growing away from its traditional academic roots. If, in the process, it grows away from a commitment to the development of new ideas and knowledge, it will lose its reason for being, but if it is committed to the development of more appropriate knowledge and methods, it will result in a great step forward. With the development of a broader conception of knowledge, a less constraining notion of the scientific method, and an awareness of the limitations of particular methods, psychology could indeed be the most important human science at the beginning of the twenty-first century.

INDEX

119

A 2
B 3
C 4
D 5
E 6
F 7
G 8
H 9
I 0
J 1